ABOUT THE AUTHOR

Brian Jones is a former Bank officia............... Adviser. Most of his adult life has been spent playing football and watching his beloved Wolverhampton Wanderers, as well as a cricket career spanning fifty-two unbroken years. After retiring from office work, he now delivers Bikeability to schoolchildren. Recreationally he is a racing cyclist, and is particularly active in Time Trials.

This book is a recounting of his early years from 1950 to 1969, and the reasons why his adult life panned out the way it did and not perhaps the way it should have. These days he lives in Surrey, cycling and singing in a church choir and a choral society.

MISSPENT YOUTH

A Warning to the Youth of Today

By BRIAN JONES

To STAN

I hope you enjoy the book!
Kind regards

OCTOBER 2020

PUBLISHED by BRIAN STUART JONES

THIS BOOK IS DEDICATED TO MOM AND DAD

Mom never did anything for me that wasn't founded in her love and devotion, and I still miss her enormously, 24 years after she had to leave us.

Dad, or the Old Man as my brother Roger and I called him, never had the chance to grow old, and this year marks the fiftieth anniversary of his unexpectedly early passing. I wish I had had longer with him. But to you both…

I'll see you in my dreams

January 2020

DISCLAIMER

This work depicts actual events in the life of the author as truthfully as recollection permits and/or can be verified by research. Occasionally, dialogue consistent with the character or nature of the person speaking has been supplemented. All persons within are actual individuals; there are no composite characters. I have intended no detriment to the characters of people still living, nor to those who have gone to a better place. The only person who has their character maligned in this book is the author himself.

ISBN no. 978-1-8380005-0-9

CONTENTS

ACKNOWLEDGMENTS

Special thanks to Mary Bodfish, respected local historian and one of the leading lights of the Smethwick Heritage Society, for her help in setting the tone for this book, proofreading, making adjustments to my grammar and punctuation to make the text an easier read and for providing valuable local information about Bearwood, Smethwick and events of the Second World War in the locality.

There is no greater authority on our beloved area than Mary, and I was fortunate enough to share a classroom with her at Bearwood Road Junior School.

Also to my great friends Trevor Boyle and Robert Gilding, who have relived our lives at Holly Lodge Grammar School over fifty years ago whenever we have met, and the warmth and friendship they have accorded me in the intervening period.

FOREWORD

In this lively memoir Brian vividly recalls life as a youngster growing up in Bearwood in the 1950s and 60s, being pulled from an early age in different directions by the attractions of sport and the demands of school and church.   To a local historian such as myself, in doing so he makes an interesting contribution to the oral history of Smethwick in the second half of the 20th century, which is very welcome. Further, as I shared the classroom at Bearwood Road School with him for several years, and also attended St Mary's Church, I can vouch for its authenticity. I must also add that even someone like myself, who hasn't a sporting bone in their body, will thoroughly enjoy sharing these memories.

Brian also reflects particularly on how his life was shaped, both through the circumstances into which he was born, and the choices he made himself in his young days. We have all asked ourselves, as Brian does here, if we had chosen otherwise at times, how different might our lives have been?   We can feel for him, for we too, when arrived at various cross-roads in our life, have often unthinkingly hurried on before we realised that a choice of pathways lay before us.

Did Brian's choices really lead him down the pathway of a misspent youth? It is for the reader to decide!

Mary Bodfish

Chapter One – Surplices, Soccer Boots and Other Sporting Distractions

The early part of my life might not be out of the ordinary, but before I indeed became a youth, my earliest recollection involved the internationally celebrated film star Julie Walters, now Dame Julia, to give her correct birth name.

She is exactly nine months to the day older than me, and her family lived in the next street to mine. The younger of Julie's two older brothers, Kevin, was in the same school class as my brother Roger from the age of 5 up to when Roger left school at 16. I remember Kevin breaking the Holly Lodge long jump record at Hadley Stadium at the school sports day, by appearing to jump off the end of the long jump pit. In later years Kevin, who was a qualified physiotherapist, became the first team trainer for my club Wolverhampton Wanderers (and Birmingham City); and coincidentally I also had him as my next-door neighbour when I bought a house in Harborne, a suburb of Birmingham.

Julie's mother, Mary, and my Mom, Margie, used to meet once a week and have a cup of tea in a tea shop on the Bearwood Road; and would, on a fine day, walk from there to Lightwoods Park Extension, sit on a bench, and let me and (Dame) Julie romp around naked on a blanket. Everyone always has a first memory and this is mine. I reckon I was two and a half at the time (Dame J three and a quarter), which makes the timeline Summer 1953. My first memory therefore was romping around naked with a film star, although as you can see, I am elasticising the facts somewhat with this claim!

When one begins a book by recounting the events of one's own life, then quite frequently the reader has to wade through the usual facts and figures ad nauseam – so let us crack on as soon as possible with this usual stuff, and get it over and done with, which probably will not distinguish this part of my recollections as out of the ordinary. Judge for yourself!

I first saw the light of day on Wednesday 22nd November 1950 at approximately 2 pm in the afternoon, in the front upstairs bedroom of our quite smart end of terrace house which Mom and Dad were to buy off the Council in the years to come. The light of day is somewhat stretching the point, as I am told it snowed on the day I was born, and the dozens of subsequent birthdays I have celebrated since have only contributed to the myth that late November ever benefits from the light of day, with its short daylight hours, and its interminably dingy weather.

However, what must have brightened my 5 year old brother Roger's day was that when he was called upstairs on his return from school to view his new sibling, I greeted him rather extrovertly by peeing when I was cradled in my mother's arms as she lay on the bed; and hitting a spot halfway up the bedroom wall. A prodigious feat for one of such tender years, sorry, minutes; and one which was probably a foretaste of my interest in sporting accomplishment.

Anyway, peeing up the wall was not, and more to the point, probably never will be, an Olympic sport. I would not be putting this dubious skill to use again until I was about ten years old at Bearwood Road Junior School when, in common with some of my classmates, we used to pee over the glassless window spaces in the boys' outdoor loo onto our unsuspecting classmates on the other side of the wall while they were playing some ball game. I never had the satisfaction of knowing whether they worked out why it appeared to have been raining out of a cloudless blue sky!

We lived in Milcote Road, in Bearwood, a reasonably presentable suburb of Smethwick, which was only just inside Staffordshire, as our road ran against the boundary of Birmingham at the far end of the road, the centre of the big city being but four short miles to the east. Birmingham was in Warwickshire in those days.

Bearwood was made up of long straight streets of late Victorian terraced houses, the residents of which were mainly local factory workers and commuters into Birmingham. There was a long shopping street, Bearwood Road, or 'the Bear' as it was known in the vicinity, which was typical of the 1950s with Woolworth's, Timothy Whites and gent's outfitters Foster Brothers as well as local butchers and greengrocers, and the Midland Red bus garage. This was the Head Office of the renowned bus company and was sited opposite St Mary's Church. Every Midland Red bus always bore an 'HA' Smethwick registration number.

I do know I had a knee problem pre-school (I was probably three years old or four at the most), because I was taken by Mom to the Birmingham Orthopaedic Hospital on Broad Street to have some sort of manipulation done to my right knee, which rather mysteriously bears a small half-inch horizontal scar to this day. This knee has never caused me the slightest problem so I can't claim any sporting aspirations or career were cut short by a chronic knee problem. I have been lucky with injuries – I just didn't do them.

Parental Influences on Me

At this point I must let it be a matter of public record that the two greatest men I ever knew were my Dad and Basil Westcott, who was the vicar at our local parish church, St Mary's. More of Basil later. Both had departed from my life by the end of my teens but their legacies will never leave me.

Dad was a man of seemingly never-ending optimism who enjoyed nothing more than a laugh and a giggle. He was a practical joker of some originality, and if he couldn't catch you verbally with one-liners such as "Did you know they never hanged a man with a wooden leg? They always used a rope!" Then he would, in his lunch hour at work, make some metallic contraption which would leap out of a book when you opened it.

He was an experienced toolmaker, and his knowledge of engineering meant that he was the Go-To man in Bearwood for anyone who had a mechanical problem with their car. He never turned anyone down; and to Mom's constant exasperation, if he wasn't in the house, he was outside in his overalls, with his head under someone's car bonnet, or he was underneath their actual motor. When my big mate Trevor Boyle bought a Ford Anglia which was held together by willpower and magnetism, Dad ensured we got down to Minehead in Somerset in it for our holiday jobs at Butlin's Holiday camp by ingenious use of, well, Sellotape. It worked. We got there and back.

Mom and Dad treated Trev like another son because he was such a likeable character, and often I would come home after doing my paper round in the evening to enquire what was for dinner, and Trev would be there, having called for me to go out that evening and reply, licking his lips, "Shepherd's Pie!", because Mom couldn't resist feeding him as well!

Whenever or wherever we went Dad carried in his inside jacket pocket a set of four ivory 'bones' which he would produce at the appropriate moment and accompany any piece of music being played, sometimes with that pursed lip bohemian-style whistling of his. It was a riot! He loved me and my brother - and Mom - like the ideal Dad, and he hardly ever missed a football or cricket match I was playing in. If he did, it was because he was doing my paper round for me to enable me to play in that day's game.

My paternal grandmother, my Dad's Mom, was from Chatham in Kent and she spoke with a Cockney accent; and although Dad was born and raised a Brummie and spoke with a Brummie accent, he used many of his mother's Cockney sayings, which meant that I hadn't a clue what he was on about half the time. He would describe someone as a "Silly sore froed 'un" of which a literal translation was presumably a 'silly, sore-throated one', and was usually directed by Dad at someone who was being, well, just plain daft. If anyone who hails from Chatham is reading this book then they are welcome to help with the idiomatic mysteries of their local accent!

At the outbreak of war in 1939 Dad worked for Birmingham Aluminium Castings Company, known to everyone as 'the Birmid'. Located in northern Smethwick in Dartmouth Road it was, like many other Smethwick firms, given over to War Office production of the hardware needed by the Allied forces. The Birmid produced aluminium castings, principally for aircraft, and specifically for the Castle Bromwich Spitfire factory. Thus Dad's was a reserved occupation, which meant that he did not have to join up; so he signed up to the Home Guard platoon which was based in Warley Woods at Warley Abbey, a large neo-gothic house used by the local golf club. He told me that he spent World War Two protecting Bearwood from the Grey Lady, who haunted the Woods from the old Abbey ruins.

Mom and Dad were married in St Mary's Church on Saturday, September 28th 1940, and as he was the first member of the Home Guard platoon to be married since its formation, his Captain insisted that he went to the altar in full uniform, despite Mom knowing nothing about this plan, and this after she had bought him a suit in which he was to be wed. Mom's thoughts on this were unprintable, and this for a woman who never swore!

Dad's account of the local 'phoney war' was not borne out by the facts, as Bearwood and Smethwick did experience several serious incidents. In November 1940 the centre of Bearwood was hit by three bombs, hitting an air raid shelter in Wattis Road, Bearwood Road School and the row of shops opposite. Another bomb came down in Abbey Road. Several people were killed.

A German Heinkel 1-11 bomber crashed onto houses in Hales Lane, Smethwick (now St Marks Road) in April 1941. The following night two hundred incendiary bombs were dropped.

In February 1942 an RAF training plane clipped the cable of a barrage balloon tethered at Avery's Sports Ground in Sandon Road, where Bearwood meets Edgbaston. The plane went on to crash at the rear of numbers 12 to 18 Park Road, Bearwood, killing the three crew members, who were believed to be Polish RAF trainees. Several fires were started by the spilt fuel and 14 Park Road was almost completely burned out, but most fortunately there was no-one home at the time.

After Hitler realised he couldn't bomb Bearwood into submission, then the later years of the war must indeed have been deadly dull for the Home Guard. The Midland Red buses from the garage were driven up to the Woods and kept there overnight to keep them safe from air-raids – not a lot of excitement in guarding them, though!

The boys in khaki therefore resorted to creating their own entertainment to keep them from screaming out loud. Therefore, on his way home from tours of duty in Warley Woods, Dad and his mates would often swap over the garden gates of houses in Upper Saint Mary's Road, as well as removing flowers from one front garden and replanting them in another to give the bewildered residents a surprise when they opened their curtains the next morning.

Dad seemed popular with everyone. I never knew him to be ill, and then one Friday in 1970 he was brought home from work all the way from Coventry because he had been sick at work. He went to bed from where he never rose, as he died of lung cancer fifteen days later in St Chad's Hospital, Edgbaston on 27th July. He was 55 years old and still in his prime. I couldn't cry at his funeral at St Mary's despite his shocking loss; I suppose I was being strong for him. His passing was a major reason why my decision-making was so poor as I grew up, as he wasn't there beside me when I would have needed his guiding hand.

Mom was a seamstress by trade, having her first job after leaving school with the well-established Birmingham City Centre firm of dressmakers called Kean & Scott. This was well before the war, and before she married Dad.

She didn't return to work until I was firmly established in school, when she took a cleaner's job at the large house belonging to the Manageress of George Baines' Bakery and Cake Shop, which was separated only by a couple of buildings from St Mary's Church on the Bearwood Road. The Manageress's house was in Westfield Road, Edgbaston, one of the most well-heeled residential roads in the area, and the same road in which the Wimbledon Ladies' Singles Champion Ann Jones has always lived since her marriage to millionaire businessman Pip Jones. So - not too shabby.

Mom 's mixing with these excellently- connected people meant that she had developed a friendship with a lady who had a lovely house in Lapal, a suburb of Halesowen which benefitted from panoramic views of the Clent Hills, a local beauty spot. She and I were invited to tea at this lady's house when I was about nine years old, and this presented logistical difficulties for both of us. For Mom, as she decided to go all Hyacinth Bucket and converse in an accent wot woz all la-di-da, much to my amusement. My problem was that I simply lacked any semblance of social skills; not surprising as my tenth birthday was some distance away.

This all came to a head some minutes after our hostess, (or her staff!) had placed a pyramid of scrummy looking sarnies on the table, which they then both ignored because they simply carried on talking to each other. I, never one to miss an opportunity, got stuck in as I was not being consulted conversationally, so ploughed on regardless. Mother had noticed my progress through the pyramid, and to hide her own embarrassment, enquired of me in a very up-market accent "Brain (sic), don't you think you've had enough sanninges?" With a quicksilver response I defended myself, telling her "But I've only had nine!" Which, although statistically accurate, was too much information, and a veritable conversation stopper. When we got outside to start the journey home, she grabbed me by the hand and 'put me in neutral' by shaking me forcibly by the wrist. "Wait till I tell your father!" she threatened, but never once followed up on her promise, much to my relief.

This was the second time I had embarrassed Mom in public, as when I was about six, she and I were walking home from one of her (interminable) shopping trips to the Bearwood Road when she bumped into an acquaintance whereupon they started talking. And talking. And talking............until I was forced to pull Mom's hand, as my arm was reaching vertically up to hers due to my lack of inches, and enquire plaintively "Mom, have you finished talking to that fat lady?" Another showstopper; and one where Mom made me see the error of my loose tongue. A career for me in the diplomatic corps was shelved that very day.

Surplices and Sporting Distractions

Meanwhile, on my eighth birthday, my parents, or chiefly my mother, had me follow in my brother's footsteps by joining the church choir at St Mary's, Bearwood as a sweet-voiced treble. My brother was already part of the choir hierarchy being Head Boy; and as his fourteenth birthday loomed on the horizon, his voice was showing signs of breaking as the mellifluous tones of his younger sibling were preparing to be launched on the unsuspecting congregation of St Mary's for the first time.

My parents were not religious per se, but I think they were God-fearing people, in particular my mother; and she insisted that my brother and I should both have a church upbringing, if for no other reason than it was a positive way of building on the discipline that school was already providing. I was not sent down the route of the Cubs and then the Scouts but joined the choir instead. The Church had thriving Scout and Girl Guide troops and coming into contact with the Brownies and the Guides was a nerve-wracking experience for this impressionable eight-year-old boy. I didn't have a sister, so girls in uniforms were, well, let's be honest, alarming!

The highlight of the choir's year was the annual Choirboys' Outing on the train to the seaside which, as we lived in Birmingham which is about as far away from the sea as you can get, this usually meant a four-hour train journey to our destination. As this was the late fifties, we were all avid train spotters like most boys at that time. We all climbed aboard the trains armed with our Ian Allan Trainspotters Manuals, and we would tick off the numbers in our books of the trains as they sped by. The crème de la crème of train engines in the 1950s were the Britannia class (numbered 70001 to about 70050, each engine named after a famous person or landmark; and I actually possessed a working train set which had 70037 Robin Hood as its engine.

We were on one outing when someone found out that 70001 Britannia itself would pass us at a certain stage, and we all eagerly awaited its arrival. No one more so than a choirboy called Jimmy, who had seen all the Brits except Britannia itself, and could not contain his excitement and anticipation as the great moment approached. Poor Jim never witnessed Britannia, because as this Rolls Royce of train engines passed majestically by, fifteen of us sat on him in the train compartment. You can imagine the impression this made on the writer, as I witnessed at first hand that there was more fun to be had by pratting about than toeing the line. More evidence in later chapters.

I was the archetypical younger brother; and on another outing, my older brother Roger was saddled with making sure that my new school cap remained firmly in place on my head. This no doubt cramped his style as he wanted to be doing outrageous things with his peers, who were of course a lot older than me. The inevitable happened, as I stuck my head out of the train window to see a spottable engine pass and my cap blew off, making it irretrievable as our train sped on. I do remember Roger being told the error of his ways by Mom when he presented his bareheaded younger brother on our return.

The vicar of St Mary's was the Reverend Basil Brooke Foss Westcott and he was in his early sixties (I am guessing) at the time I joined the choir in November 1958. Basil's incumbency at St Mary's was from 1948 to 1965.

He was a bachelor and shared the vicarage with his twin sister Rosemary, who kept house for him. He had a deep and lasting effect on the lives of a whole generation of lads and young men in Bearwood; and is remembered with not only respect but affection.

He possessed the most booming voice with which he delivered sermons of great authority from the pulpit. A bald-headed man of tiny stature, he made up for it with this voice of stentorian magnificence, which inspired all who were privileged to hear him.

He was the grandson of a famous man, the Bishop of Durham, Brook Fosse Westcott and to me he was God's representative. He taught me many lessons in life which I should have heeded more; and his frequent visits to our house were usually done to report to my parents on the progress of my older brother and I as we made our way in the church. When I was confirmed at the age of fourteen, I attended Basil's confirmation classes weekly and I still remember his teaching on what the Holy Sacrament actually meant.

During his visits to our house he would sprawl across our settee, his tiny frame filling the available space with an arm draped backwards over one of the sides and a leg over the far side, as he stretched his length fully.   My Dad, who didn't attend Church, always welcomed him to our sitting room with the words "Fancy a tot, Vic?", and that was the only time I saw the whisky bottle opened.

When Basil left St Mary's to take up his final appointment at the Woolpit Rectory, in Bury St Edmunds, Suffolk, I made a special visit to what had seemed like previously unreachable East Anglia to visit him.   Finally, he returned to the Midlands in his well-deserved retirement to the Severnside Worcestershire village of Hallow, deep in Elgar territory. (Please note that like me, Sir Edward Elgar was a Wolves supporter, and used to ride his bike from Worcester to the Molineux Ground in the centre of Wolverhampton for home matches). Basil eventually ended his life at Hallow, but not before I had paid this wonderful man one final visit. I like to think that Dad and Basil (or Fred and Vic) these days share a tot upstairs in HQ.

One crossed Basil at one's peril, and I learned a salutary lesson one Tuesday night at Choirboy's club after choir practice. Choirboy's Club consisted of playing snooker on a small table or table tennis on a full-sized table, in one of the church rooms at the verger's house adjoining the church hall after choir practice on a Tuesday. I was engaged in a game of ping pong doubles with Basil on the opposing side; a disputed point arose, and I uttered the words "Cheats never prosper!" which prompted an explosion from Basil, about how I should never accuse anyone of being a cheat.

The game ended there and then as Basil's tirade left a lesson ringing in my ears, which to this day I have never forgotten. The lasting outcome of that little episode is that I have never accepted cheating of any form in any sport since that day, and I use the actual word 'cheat' sparingly and with great reluctance.

Weddings at St Mary's provided an early taste of the conflict between sporting and more sensible activities which was to dog my footsteps throughout my youth. Although we were remunerated in a small way as choirboys, attendance at weddings on Saturdays was a real source of income, as sometimes up to four services could be arranged on one Saturday. The choirboys, of whom only the eight most senior of those available could sing in the choir, were paid the princely sum of two shillings and sixpence (12.5p) for each ceremony. Two and six, or half a crown, or even more colloquially half a dollar, which dated from the time when the US dollar was worth five shillings, or four dollars to the pound sterling (those were the days!), was serious money to the choristers.

Some wedding Saturdays I found myself playing football for Bearwood Road School, a three mile bus ride away in West Smethwick Park, with a ten o'clock kick off time; then jump on the 221 bus which conveniently stopped right outside the gate to St Mary's Church, dash into the vestry, don my pristine choir robes and take my place, to provide the angelic accompaniment to some blissfully happy couple's big day.

That happiness would have been somewhat marred, because if I had hitched up my cassock a little to my thighs then they would have seen me still wearing my Bearwood Road football kit and covered from head to toe in cloying West Smethwick Park mud. There were no showers available at that ghastly arena of football, nor any time for me to get home and scrubbed clean and make it to the church on time.

If we did have four weddings to get through on one Saturday (no there wasn't a funeral, that came later in a film) then Basil would ensure that the strict timetable was adhered to. If for example, in wedding one, the bride exercised her time-honoured right to turn up late, then that would start to get us behind schedule, and the knock-on effect of her tardiness could impact on the rest of the day. Wedding two might have the spectacle of the bride, or even sometimes the groom, fainting, or plainly and simply bursting into tears, which used to cause a further delay. Wedding three might see the bride's mother suddenly bursting into an uncontrollable fit of hysteria, which meant that Wedding Four's participants might be standing at the back of the church before wedding three had cleared itself out.

Basil had a simple and effective remedy for all this shilly-shallying and sabotaging of his timetable. He would simply enunciate each wedding ceremony quicker and quicker, so that couple number four didn't have time to faint, cry or collapse before Basil was pronouncing them man and wife, and they possibly didn't realise what had just hit them. And so we all got home in time for the football results; with our pockets richer to the tune of ten bob. Not to be sniffed at, as today its equivalent would probably represent the deposit on a condominium in the Caribbean.

My brother, the Head Chorister, at the Choirboys' Christmas party shortly before his fifteenth birthday announced to Basil that, as his voice was breaking, he would be leaving the trebles and re-joining the choir as a bass after a short sabbatical. The Choirboys' Christmas Party basically comprised a food binge and several rounds of British Bulldog, a roughhouse of a game which was an excuse for the older boys to annihilate the younger boys: a little like Rugby without a ball.

The survivors were allowed to continue their lives and celebrate Christmas with their families. I hated British Bulldog. I never enjoyed being smashed to a pulp by some fat lump whose only sporting prowess was, well, that he was a fat lump. Rugby will not be mentioned again in this tome. Whereupon, Basil relayed my brother's decision to the assembled choir and paid a glowing and extensive tribute to his service to the choir.

When my time arrived I thought this was the way to go, so one month after my own fourteenth birthday, and at the same event, I made the same announcement to Basil that as I now could only sing treble with the assistance of Extra Strong mints, it was now appropriate to announce my forthcoming departure from the Choir. I waited for the glowing tributes. Basil reacted by telling me in no uncertain terms that I was not leaving the choir and was going to have to soldier on. The balloon that was my ego burst instantly! This probably influenced my decision not to re-join the choir as a bass in the fulness of time – a decision I have come to regret as the years have rolled by. A pattern was starting to emerge in my decision-making processes.

School & Sporting Distractions

I started at Bearwood Road Primary School on the first Thursday in January 1956 in the Baby Class, or Year One as it would be styled in the modern era. The biro hadn't really caught on at this time, and a class of fifty (yes, fifty!) little horrors were too high risk to be let loose as the older children in the school were with steel pens and inkwells; so we were issued, not with paper and pencil, but a rectangular piece of slate and a stick of white chalk. I must have been something of a prodigy, because when we were asked to write the numerals nought to nine on the little chalkboards, most of my classmates had to be shown how to achieve this.

But I already wrote in Times New Roman; and I remember our teacher, an elderly spinster (the term used to describe unmarried women rather ungraciously in those days) called Miss Padfield, correcting my numeral threes because I had used a straight top instead of a curly one. As most of the rest of the class couldn't actually make contact with the board using their chalks, I had her marked down as a pedant from day one!

I am not sure where this progress or talent had come from, as my sainted mother was, on her own admission, no academic; although my Dad, Fred, was by now a skilled toolmaker with Armstrong Siddeley, the up-market car manufacturers in Coventry, and he did have some dexterity with numbers, as the backs of most of his fag packets bore testimony. Armstrong Siddeley was later bought by Rolls-Royce Aeroengines, and he made his contribution to the building of the prototype Concorde aeroplane before his dreadful demise from lung cancer at the brutally early age of 55.

Whilst my classmates were, basically, learning to write, I would be placed in an ante-room with an exercise book and a pencil (yes technology was moving along at an alarming rate), where I would compose short stories which were deemed good enough to read out to the rest of the class. I am not going to surprise you all with a compendium of these works but I could have been a budding six-year-old Ian Fleming, and no mistake!

This rapid rise through infant and junior schools began to gather pace at breakneck speed, and by the age of eight I was moved (along with two other September-born classmates, Peter and John) up a year so that we missed out the second year of the junior school and went straight into the third -year class of Miss Thorpe. It is no exaggeration to say that the three of us not only coped with this promotion admirably, but actually stood out in the year above. I was now on my way. The sky really was the limit. I remember we had the fourth-year spelling exam where we had to spell one hundred words enunciated by our teacher, another unmarried gel called Miss Pretty.

As an aside, it was put to me that these women teachers, who were all around sixty years old, had survived the First World War, unlike their boyfriends, and had dedicated themselves to the teaching profession instead of marrying someone else and raising another generation of little Herberts and Herberthas. We were exceptionally fortunate in being taught by Miss Gwen Pretty and Miss Isabel Thorpe – they were outstandingly good teachers, with a very high success rate in getting these enormous baby-boomer generation classes through the Eleven Plus and giving them a solid foundation for work at a grammar school.

Anyway, back to the spelling exam. I recorded an erudite 99 and failed only on the word 'separate' which I disappointingly spelt with the letter 'e' instead of the first 'a'. I was mortified. That word still haunts me!

The time came for the nemesis event of most kids in the early 1960s – the Eleven Plus School Examination! This determined a scholar's future path, because by passing this examination one could go to either the Grammar School or the Technical School. Failure condemned one to the Secondary Modern School route. I think successive governments missed a serious trick with children's education by creating the Comprehensive School system, which basically removed the aforementioned distinction and effectively abolished the Eleven Plus exam itself.

Because the three of us who had been promoted at Bearwood Road Juniors were a year ahead of our time we were officially too young to enter the Eleven Plus, but some bright spark in the Education Department allowed my September-born classmates Peter and John to take the exam, yet they refused me. They of course flew through the exam, and duly went to the Grammar School, even though they were from the year below, and there they remained right through to the end of Sixth form. They even went to University a year early!

This was all explained to me at the time and although I had to swallow the decision, I didn't realise the long-term effects this was going to have on me. It was a major reason why I drifted towards sport instead of Academia.

I was reunited therefore with my erstwhile classmates in the top class of the Junior school; and I stagnated for a year as I sat through the whole final year again. Although boredom set in I still managed to finish top of the class in the internal exams; and I was told, although I can't remember by whom, that my Eleven Plus ranking was fourth in the whole County Borough, which contained 12 Junior Schools, with about a thousand eleven year olds entering the exam.

In due course, on Thursday 6th September 1962, a day in which the heavens dumped an astonishing quantity of rain on us new entrants, or 'fags' as we were known by our seniors, I entered Holly Lodge Grammar School for Boys, in Smethwick. When it was founded in the 1920s it was grandly-named Holly Lodge County Grammar School. The school had a great reputation for academic achievement and much to my interest, sporting achievement. It was at about this time that my under-utilised brain started making all the wrong decisions; and my youth was about to be seriously misspent.

Chapter Two – Football and Me

If you were born and brought up in England in the immediate post-war years, as I was, then football was bred into your consciousness. The austerity of the immediate peacetime period was offset, for the working classes at least, by the diversion of football, and the English Football League system, consisting of 4 divisions comprising 92 clubs, meant that almost every nook and cranny of the land was in the catchment area of one, or in a lot of cases, several professional football teams. The resumption of league football after VE Day in 1945 was greeted by record crowds as the masses saw football as their new passion – a complete change from the interminable struggle against the tyranny of Hitler and the Nazis.

Where I lived was not unusual in terms of football club geography. Our house was 3 miles from West Bromwich Albion. 6 miles from both Aston Villa and Birmingham City, 10 miles from Walsall, 12 miles from Wolverhampton Wanderers and 23 miles from Coventry City, the place where my Dad worked. He had four older brothers who all supported WBA, so not to be outdone, he hoisted his flag with Aston Villa. Now when I was growing up, the Villa were perennially moderate, pausing once to emerge from this mediocrity by winning the FA Cup in 1957, beating the pre-Munich Busby Babes of Manchester United at Wembley in the final which I watched from my sickbed as I was laid low with measles so my dad and brother brought the telly upstairs to my bedroom.

I do however remember watching the previous year's Cup Final on the telly when in 1956 Manchester City put another of our local teams to the sword, Birmingham City, by 3 goals to one, despite Manchester City's German goalkeeper Bert Trautmann, who was a former prisoner-of-war in Britain, breaking his neck in the second half! He carried on to the end as well, no wonder we took six years to defeat him and his mates in the aforementioned conflagration!

My other great memory of this final was of the local evening newspaper the Birmingham Mail publishing cartoon caricatures of each of the Birmingham City, or the Blues as they were nicknamed, players in readiness for the Final. I collected these avidly, sticking them in one of my many long-lost scrap books (which would now be worth a fortune incidentally). The one I remember the most was that of the Blues right back Jeff Hall, who tragically died of polio some two years later. This had a vivid effect on me when I reached eight years old, as it was probably the first time I had seen a living person before they died.

The four major clubs in our locality, Villa, Blues, WBA and Wolves all played at that time in the late fifties in the First Division, the top tier of English football, so to avoid fixture chaos Blues and WBA would be at home on one Saturday and Villa and Wolves would be at home on the next. My Dad would always go to a game every Saturday and would visit each of the four grounds regularly.

When I was old enough to be sneaked under the turnstiles with my Dad sticking a few coppers by way of a bribe to the gateman to get me in cheaper, I started going to games with him. The first match I ever went to was in September 1956 to see Blues (fresh from their Cup Final mauling) defeat Preston North End by 3 goals to nil in front of a crowd of the size Blues can only dream of nowadays, 44458. A free-scoring forward named Alex Govan scored a hat-trick for Blues on that day.

I would then turn up at school the following Monday and recount in true football reporter style all the details of the match I had been to, and I was starting to develop an interest and knowledge of the game which belied my tender years.

I used to talk a lot about football to a classmate named Clive Parkes, who was a Blues fan and whose interest and knowledge of the game was every bit as developed as mine. So much so that on the morning of Friday February 7th 1958, the seven-year-old Clive and I stood solemnly at the start of the day in the school cloakroom listing all the Manchester United players who had been killed in the Munich Air Crash on the previous day.

We discussed with the deepest gravitas like two elderly gentlemen the ending of the lives and careers of these players, who not only were nearly all in the England team, but were also the champion team of England at the time. The Munich Air Disaster is one of those moments where everyone can recall what they were doing and where they were when they heard about it (like the assassination of JFK, which happened on my thirteenth birthday, the 9/11 massacre in USA, or the death of Princess Diana).

This event resonated through the whole of the nation, and contributes massively as to why Manchester United draw support from all over the country, indeed the globe. Some ten or twelve days later Duncan Edwards died of his injuries sustained in the crash and England had lost not only its greatest footballer, aged 21, but he was also a local lad from Dudley, snatched by Manchester United from under the noses of Wolves. He is still revered to this day with a statue in Dudley marketplace, and would probably have captained England in its victorious World Cup Final in 1966 when he would still have been only in his twenties.

There was another lad in our class called Robert Millward, who lived close to me in Lightwoods Road, and we used to walk to and from school together. Robert, or Rob as he was known, was football daft like me, taking his place alongside me in the school football team and we used to amuse ourselves on our school walks by repeating the previous Saturday's Five o'clock Sports Report radio programme parrot-fashion. We would go to each other's houses and watch the sport on the telly and then we discovered the joys of that prince of football games, Subbuteo.

Birthdays and Christmas would see our stock of Subbuteo accessories grow and great matches took place on that lovely green baize Subbuteo football pitch, complete with commentary and crowd noises. We became walking encyclopaedias on sport in general, and football in particular. Sadly, when Rob was fourteen, he developed rheumatic fever which curtailed his sporting participation somewhat but I feel that I had been instrumental in giving him a lifelong love of sport.

So much so, that he eventually graduated to being the principal Football reporter for the world-renowned AP Reuter's News Agency. During the 2010 World Cup in South Africa Rob filed his after match report on one of the Semi Finals on his laptop and then retired to his hotel bedroom as usual, but when he didn't emerge for breakfast the next morning he was found to have passed away in the night at the age of 59. I like to think I helped sow the seeds of a very successful journalistic career in sport. He was a very popular and hugely respected guy, judging by the tributes paid to him.

Before Subbuteo, my mania for football manifested itself in the use of my collection of about three hundred glass marbles. These were divided into teams, usually by colour, and a lot of the marbles had individual names. The marbles played league games on our sitting room carpet, albeit propelled by my hand movements, and the Red team were all-conquering. They provided most of the England Marble team, which played representative international matches against teams of other unsuspecting marbles. Subbuteo arrived and rescued me from this marble world which no-one else inhabited.

I also had leagues which I chronicled in exercise books, where the previous Saturday's actual football scores in the First Division would be torn up by me and thrown into a hat to be drawn out FA Cup style. So, if Wolves had scored two on the Saturday for example, they would be pulled out of the hat with two goals and then they would 'play' against the next team drawn out with their Saturday score. If the Chairman of the Football League position had become vacant in 1962, I believe I would have got it after interview at the age of eleven, without a shadow of a doubt!

Here is a date that is etched firmly into my personal legend – Saturday 31st January 1959. How so? Well, as previously chronicled, my Dad was an Aston Villa fan, and they did nothing to entice supporters like him to go and witness their repeated ritual humiliation at the hands of just about every other club in the division.

As Aston Vanilla (so-called because they got licked every week – comic genius) played at home at the same time as the Wolves, he would therefore go and watch Wolves play to spare himself the pain of watching the Villa.

At this time Wolves were indisputably the best club in England, because they seemed to batter every team they played against; scoring over one hundred league goals four years in succession during this period. I believe no other club has achieved this feat even two years in a row.

I accompanied him, therefore, to the Wolves ground Molineux on 31.01.59 whereupon they sent Blackburn Rovers packing to the tune of 5 goals to nil. I thought this was brilliant. The sight of those old gold shirts bearing down at pace on the opposition goal was something I could not resist, and I was present over the next two or three seasons as Manchester City and Fulham were hit for 9 goals and WBA 7. So deep down I became a Wolves supporter. In that season of my first Molineux visit (1958-59) Wolves won the League Championship and the following season (1959-60) were runners-up to Burnley by one point in the league and despatched the hapless Blackburn Rovers 3-0 in the FA Cup Final. I told you they were good!

I went to hundreds of games over the next few years – with my Dad, on my own, or with my mates and I came to know each of the four grounds intimately. The Blues ground, St Andrews, with its pre-war shabbiness never inspired me greatly, as the football snob in me took hold. West Brom was a similar ground, but with my mates I managed to get into some of its more exclusive parts, and because it was the most local ground it held some sort of allure.

I stood against the front wall by the halfway line and watched at pitch level as Villa's centre forward Gerry Hitchens stormed through the West Brom defence twice to give them a 2-0 victory one year. Shortly after he was off to Italy and Internazionale Milan from where he became a star and never returned to play in this country.

I stood behind the goal at a sparsely attended West Brom reserve game on another occasion, when the West Brom left winger Geoff Carter let rip with a pile driver which swerved past the goal only to be caught cleanly by the eleven-year-old me. Unfortunately, without realising it, when I caught the ball, all the money fell out of my gloves and I was refused admission onto the bus after the game, so had to endure a three-mile walk home in the dark.

Villa Park was palatial, and was a regular venue of FA Cup semi-finals, for which my Dad always managed to get me a ticket. I stood on the Holte End in 1964 for the semi-final between Preston and Swansea as a 13- year-old among 72,000 spectators, and was offered a sip of whisky from a disillusioned Swansea supporter after he had watched the Preston centre half Tony Singleton lob the keeper from 45 yards to send Preston to the Wembley final.

But Molineux enthralled me. You could walk into the place and touch the atmosphere. I never got near to going on the pitch, nor into the seated area. But it had this tangible atmosphere to it. The Molineux Street stand, built down the gradient of a steep hill which ran the length of the touchline, had a pitch side wall only three inches high and many was the time the centre half, Wolves or otherwise, would put the opposing centre forward into the second row of seats unceremoniously. I remember Wolves' David Woodfield doing just that to one no.9, but unfortunately the referee on the day had no sense of humour and duly sent him off!

I felt butterflies in my tummy whenever I entered the place, or even when I saw the towering floodlight pylons at Molineux's town centre site as we approached the ground. Four pylons of 48 lights, and I swear they were the biggest in the land. How you could play in this arena without being inspired by its history and enormity was beyond me. I remember watching the FA Cup replay between Wolves and Villa lying on the wall at the top of the turnstile block, after both Dad and I were defeated by the full house signs.

I saw the whole game which ended in another draw before going to West Brom's ground The Hawthorns the following Monday for the second replay, where Wolves powered home 3-nil in their new all gold kit with a Hughie McIlmoyle hat-trick. Every barnstorming goal was greeted by a deafening roar from the Wolves fans as Villa were finally put away. The all-gold kit was sensational. The gold shorts were the best thing I had ever seen in a football strip, and the Wolves looked magnificent, particularly under floodlights where this kit glowed. I swear people became Wolves fans simply because of the kit.

Mom and Dad always enjoyed their holidays and at Easter or October half term we would shoot off to Blackpool where I watched a few games at their Bloomfield Road ground. I saw Blackpool lose at home to Blackburn in a Lancashire derby, then lose to the aristocratic Everton side, who were League champions at the time, and by great coincidence lose against Wolves who although they won were now becoming a fading force.

Not as bad as Blackpool who, after they sold the fledgling and future World Cup winner Alan Ball to Everton, went into a spiralling dive through the divisions, foreshadowing Wolves' own nosedive a few years later. But being at Blackpool and seeing games between two teams who were not from the Birmingham area was like stepping onto the moon. On the way home Dad would always drive through Liverpool, which was another increasingly dominant football hotbed, and again I could sense the footballing atmosphere simply by gazing out of the car window.

I went to Wembley Stadium in April 1962 with my junior school, Bearwood Road, to see the schoolboy International. England's Under 15 Schoolboy team played a game each year at Wembley in front of 98,000 yelling schoolboys. This particular game saw England, captained by future Manchester City star Glyn Pardoe, defeat West Germany 2 goals to nil, and the Under-15 age group was to play a large part in my own footballing journey just four years after this game.

My abiding memory was turning up at Wembley Park Station (or was it Wembley Central?) on the train, and seeing a teeming mass of people, mostly schoolboys, making their way on foot to the Stadium. This was also the pre-World Cup Wembley Stadium in its original 1923 form. May I state that it was not a pretty sight, but at least I had been there, to the place where the Cup Finals were held and where England played nearly all of their internationals when at home.

I look back at that era in footballing terms, usually through the medium of You Tube on the internet, and I can't believe how slow and skill-less the game seemed to be then. I don't mean to be unkind, but the game was played on mudheaps by men who were nowhere near as fit or as quick as today's players, and there were no discernible tactics, other than a desire to get the ball closer to the opposition's goal than their own by any means possible.

The players looked like middle-aged men compared to today's young superbly honed athletes. Don't get me wrong, the game has evolved massively, as have other sports, and I have welcomed that progression. When in the 1950s defenders would toe poke the ball anywhere to get the ball safe, more often than not by giving it straight back to the opposition, then today's players retain possession of the ball jealously and with ever-increasing levels of skill.

Strikers these days propel the ball into the net with feats of athleticism which are light years ahead of when I started watching the game. It beggars belief that players with the outrageous skills of, to name but two, Lionel Messi and Cristiano Ronaldo, who have both passed the 700 goal career mark with, in 2020, no obvious signs that they are slowing up, would not have scored fifteen to twenty goals individually per game if they could be transported to 1956 with their present day skill sets. But as spectators and players we all evolve with the game.

I remember when Johann Cruyff performed what came to be known as the Cruyff turn on the world stage for the first time some forty years or so ago and we marvelled at such a feat of athletic ball-playing skill.

Nowadays, or even back in the mid-1990s my son, who was born in 1982, could not get into a local Under-10 team unless he could perform the Cruyff turn. Fortunately, he could.

I became a keen student of the game, and my ever-increasing knowledge meant that I also had a thirst for memorabilia, which led me into the hobby of collecting football programmes. My Dad would bring me programmes from each Coventry City home game, which his workmates had bought for him, (or really me); and every time I went to a game at one of the Big Four clubs, I would scour the stadia before they were tidied up after the matches for discarded programmes under the seats or on the terraces.

Then one day a lad in our class named Martin Saunders turned up at school with a battered suitcase which was crammed with programmes going back as far as 1945. There must have been two to three hundred at least in this case, and they covered teams from the whole country. I paid him a ridiculously small amount of cash for this collection and I had now acquired a valuable hoard. I added to this collection over the next year or two and then inexplicably sold the whole lot to someone else at school for a pittance.

When I look back and think that any programme which pre-dates 1960 is nowadays worth a small fortune on its own (and I had dozens of them!) I shudder to think how much they would have been worth in later years had I held on to them. This was not going to be the last barmy decision I was to make as my youth was moving on.

Chapter Three – Football at Primary School

My Dad Fred was a decent footballer. I don't know who he played for, as his career was probably long over by the time I started school, when he was already 41. I believe he was a goalkeeper, a belief based on no facts whatsoever, but he loved nothing better than to showcase his own skills by fooling around on the ball with that gangly, bony kneed gait of his. He fooled around because one of his particular heroes was the Sunderland, Newcastle and England inside forward Len Shackleton, known as the 'Clown Prince of Soccer'.

Shackleton, never one to hold back either on or off the pitch, famously wrote a book which contained a chapter called 'The Average Director's Knowledge About Football' which was humorously and somewhat predictably followed by a blank page! Dad eulogised about many of the ball playing schemers (or attacking midfielders in today's parlance), and another of his favourite players was the Northern Irishman Peter Doherty who scored 200 goals in 400 League games for a variety of clubs. My love of football was in my Dad's genes and I was very much his father's son.

Unlike, mysteriously, my brother. He was a good footballer, and was by trade a goalkeeper, representing the School 2nd XI, and even heading home a corner kick during a House Match at School when he ventured upfield from his goal to notch one in a 22-0 humbling of Kenilworth House by Warwick House. I say mysteriously, because he appeared not to have any great passion for the game, and certainly no discernible conversation on the topic.

His preferences lay elsewhere, on two wheels on the velodrome, as well as his singing in the church choir, making model aeroplanes and trainspotting. His favourite player was Tom Finney, the Preston Plumber, a one-club man who served his beloved Preston North End for 20 years.

It was fashionable to try and demonstrate one's knowledge of football by claiming that Finney was a better player than Stanley Matthews, the real legend of English football at the time. I don't know. They were different players, although I will concede that Finney was more versatile than Stan and was a goal scorer as well as a provider. There: I've just convinced myself, I think. Judge for yourself on You Tube. These days both players would simply have the ball taken off them by athletic full backs, instead of their old reliance on hypnotising the opposition into not laying a glove on them or the ball. I repeat. Judge for yourself.

On Friday 15th December 1956 Mom and I were busily engaged in making Christmas decorations out of coloured tissue paper and putting the finished articles underneath the four-legged stool on which we were working, when Dad walked in with a tiny and beautiful three month old kitten, a lovely tortoise shell girl cat who Mom immediately named Chessie.

Chessie Jones stayed with us for thirteen years, being an intrinsic part of our family, until one day she mysteriously disappeared during a spell of about twelve months when three or four cats went, never to be seen again, from our close neighbourhood. Heart-breaking naturally, but annoying as well. Chessie announced her arrival by shyly secreting herself under the stool because she was a bit overawed by her new environment, and weeing in fright all over our completed festive offerings. Shades of my arrival for my brother on the 22nd November 1950!

Chessie became an accomplice in my obsession with sport as she used to act as a goalkeeper by waiting in the recess underneath our sideboard in the sitting room and pouncing on a table tennis ball as I attempted to roll it past her on the slippery lino. She would paw the ball to safety as it reached her with all the agility of a top-class goalkeeper. If I projected this ball down to the square of lino by the kitchen door, she hurtled after it, losing her footing on the shiny floor covering and crashing with her back into the kitchen door and spinning a full three sixty degrees before coming to a dazed rest, prompting Mom to ask from the kitchen what the commotion was all about. It was only me putting Chessie through her paces!

With Chessie's ability as a goalie, I can see now why human custodians are nicknamed 'The Cat' when they fling themselves all over the place. I was a naïve young lad when Chessie blessed our lives but as I grew older, I learned to give her the love and respect she needed. It was indeed a dark day when we realised she was gone, as she had a few more summers left in her.

She did have one or two health problems, principally something wrong with her ears, called canker. From the vet we obtained some powder for this ailment, and administering it with a tin which one had to squeeze so that it pumped the stuff in to her ears was a nightmare, because you had to hold on to her as she struggling to escape your vice-like grip, as she knew what was coming. It was about as easy as rubbing ointment onto a grasshopper! She was always washing and scratching her ears as they must have been a source of constant irritation to her and she had the habit of walking around for several minutes with one of her ears inside out and flat to her head, gormlessly oblivious to the hysterics she was giving everyone!

She could also open the kitchen door to the backyard from the inside, by jumping up onto the handle and swinging on it as the door slowly opened; although she never mastered the art of backheeling the door shut, which on a cold winter's day was a less endearing trait.

Chessie also kept me amused for hours by falling asleep on top of the towels Mom had placed to dry on top of the paraffin heater in the kitchen, and as she quite audibly snored herself into a dream-laden deep slumber, would then proceed to fall off as the towels incxorably slid towards the edge of the heater with the gentle gyration of her sleeping frame. Rest in peace, my beautiful little Chessie.

Redirecting the topic to human footballers, brother Roger did however play for a Sunday League Youth team in the Parks League called Midvale United. They were quite staggeringly moderate from what I can remember.

Roger didn't play in goal all the time for them. Sometimes they used a marvellously eccentric guy named Dave Strode as custodian. Now Strode was unusual amongst his goalkeeping contemporaries in that he wore glasses whilst keeping the opposition at bay. Strode wore strange football boots as well, in that when they were wet, they appeared to exude beetroot juice. It was a most unpleasant sight. One day the ref didn't show, evidently deciding that officiating at a Midvale United fixture was not going to be a beneficial career move.

So my Dad took over and refereed the match, which was interesting, because as a player he was up to all sorts of skulduggery on the pitch; such as carrying a safety pin about his person which he would open and jab into the opposing centre forward's arse when marking him at a corner. He passed that tip on to me and most of my mates.

Anyway, this match was played on a pitch where most of the penalty area made the Somme look like the Kalahari Desert and Strode, (remember him?), lost his glasses during a goalmouth melee. "Stop the game, I've dropped me specs!" was Strode's plaintive cry, whereupon Dad ordered everyone to stand still like statues while he himself searched the goal area for Strode's optical accessories. Dad, like a good'un, found the missing lunettes when he trod on them, and Strode was duly reacquainted with his glasses which were now in several pieces. History does not record how well he performed for the rest of the match.

I was about 9 or 10 at the height of Midvale United's notoriety, and attended most matches along with my Dad. My highlight was joining in the pre-match kickabout with the big boys. One Sunday my Mom, whose knowledge of sport was that it was an event which created washing, sent me to this particular game in a brand new, light grey gaberdine mac.

I duly took my place as the self-appointed Midvale mascot for the kickabout, and the ball eventually appeared enticingly in front of me. I took a swing at the ball, only to be let badly down by my standing foot, which slipped in the morass of the goalmouth, dumping me on my backside in a huge mudpuddle. The brand new, light grey gaberdine mac now looked like it had been used to clean out a cowshed, and I spent an apprehensive couple of hours before we got home, where my Dad typically tried to defuse the situation by convulsing with laughter whilst recounting the event to my mother. She wasn't swayed by my Dad's raconteur skills, and duly went barmy at me, with some justification.

On Saturday 22nd November 1958, my eighth birthday, Mom and Dad bought me one of the new white plastic footballs which were revolutionising football in the parks for nippers like me, whereupon I sped on foot, on my own, the half mile to the football pitches of Lightwoods Park Extension, (the scene of my naked romps with Julie Walters!) and promptly started banging repeatedly this beautiful, pristine sphere into the empty goal net. This appeared to be the natural thing to do, and would eventually develop into whatever predatory instinct I might have later on as a striker.

I spent ages doing this until I was approached by a youth, who I guess was in his mid-teens, and who suggested that my life would be improved immeasurably if I handed my birthday present to him. Naturally I refused his kind offer which presented me with a dilemma: – either give my ball to this youth or allow him, as he seemed to suggest, to rip my head off and insert the ball into the resultant orifice.

Possession of the ball suddenly seemed to take on a tactical importance which was ahead of its time, so I prudently declined his offer and turned to hotfoot it home, hoping against hope that I could outpace and outlast him. Perhaps this was where my turn of speed had its genesis – I wasn't the quickest around, but I was far from the slowest. I made it home with head still attached and this ball worked overtime for me, until one day inevitably it punctured, probably after I drove it into a tree in Lightwoods Park. I hadn't yet learnt to keep the ball down when taking a snapshot at goal.

I was now approaching getting into the school football team, and at the start of the next academic year, the second year of the juniors, I played in every game for the team, which comprised boys mostly two years older than me – as were the opposition. I can't remember in which position I played, but I suspect it was in an advanced position although I don't remember scoring any goals. When the end of season photoshoot took place, we were told in the morning to present ourselves as tidily as possible that afternoon. As I used to go home at lunch time so that I could let my Mom tickle me to death, I told her about the photoshoot whereupon she emptied a jar of Brylcreme onto my hair and embellished me with a parting, which was ramrod straight.

I duly presented myself in the playground for the team shot only to be given two pieces of news. One was that the usual goalkeeper was absent through illness and secondly that I was to don the goalkeeper's jumper for the photographer. I was not only the youngest player in the team but also the shortest, so when I took my appointed place for the photo where all goalkeepers stood in the middle of the back row, I was dwarfed by the giant defenders around me; and also you can't see me, because the lad in front of me on the front row was taller than me sitting down. This photo remains one of my most humorous for the foregoing reasons.

Bearwood Road Primary School Football Team played in what to me was an iconic strip. Pea green and white striped shirts, navy blue shorts and green and white hooped socks. By pulling on that heavy, striped shirt made one feel as though one had arrived in football. I loved the kit because it meant I was representing something. In what was a drab era, where colour seemed to be drained out of everything, in retrospect the schools played in some fairly eye-catching colours.

Our local rivals Abbey Road played in royal blue and gold stripes. Uplands in bright red and green stripes. Waterloo Road, I think, played in maroon shirts, while Crocketts Lane played in yellow shirts with black sleeves. St Philips played in royal blue and white stripes, I think, as did St Matthews.

Corbett Street were adorned in blue and white quartered shirts, a la Bristol Rovers, whilst Albion School, named because the school was directly opposite the main stand of The Hawthorns, home of West Bromwich Albion, to everyone's amusement and confusion played in Arsenal shirts, red with white sleeves. Nobody told them that WBA played in navy blue and white stripes! Or a member of staff was an Arsenal supporter and was somewhat labouring the point.

The following season saw me with a year's experience in my boots and I duly played in every game that season too, with and against boys a year older than me this time. Again, probably as an attacker, and again, I don't recall scoring any goals.

I did however have a misguided belief in my own prowess, so much so that I wrote a letter to West Bromwich Albion (what? I hear Wolves fans everywhere asking) requesting a trial as I figured that at the age of ten it was the shortest bus ride to becoming an actual playing First Division footballer. I thought no more about this until a letter arrived, addressed to me, and on WBA headed notepaper. Their Manager at the time was a seasoned Scotsman called Archie Macaulay and he let me down gently but didn't close the door in the future by telling me to keep training. Still, their loss.

My time finally arrived the following season when I was at last in the top year of the junior school and I was appointed captain of the football team, principally because I had played in every match in the previous two seasons; but also because I spoke about the game like the Manager of the England team, "Wintry Walterbotty", as Professor Stanley Unwin intriguingly called Walter Winterbottom. We did well too, winning about as many as we lost in the twelve school Smethwick Primary Schools League. Each school played all the other schools once, and there was a knockout Cup. We didn't win the Cup but I exploded on to the goal scene reaching a double figure tally with ease. VAR would have ruled out one of my more spectacular efforts when we played, I think Crocketts Lane School in Victoria Park.

Victoria Park had no goal nets, and some bright spark had leant his bike against an upright with a wheel either side of the post. I burst through the Crocketts Lane defence, taking a through ball in my stride, and lashing a vicious shot goalward. Unfortunately, the ball went the wrong side of the post; but such was the power of my shot that the ball bounced energetically off the spokes of the bike wheel, rebounding back into my path whereupon, without breaking stride I smashed it high into the absent net for a quite magnificent but ultimately illegal goal. Or so I thought – the referee gave the goal and subsequently threatened to report most of the Crocketts Lane team to their Headmaster for dissent as they protested long and hard that the bike wheel had claimed an unlikely assist. It would have been a shame to disallow such a wonderful, all-action strike. Lesson learnt? Play to the whistle.

Me and my strike partner Phil Junkin, who was a year younger than me, scored about thirty goals together that season, but neither of us were invited to the trial for the Smethwick Primary Schools representative team. My biggest mate Trev Boyle (who I wasn't to meet until we went to the Grammar School) from Waterloo Road School, nailed down the number 9 shirt I seem to recall, which I can understand because he was to develop into a midfield / wide player of the silkiest skills as we moved into our teens. The main goalscoring duties were given to a scrawny kid from Uplands called Clive Milsom, who was small, wiry, bandy legged and squirmy in the box but he knew where the goal was, if he didn't know where his hankie was, as he seemed to play every game with rivers of snot running down his face.

In the playground at Bearwood Road we underwent our training for the football team by having impromptu games during morning playtime (15 minutes) or lunch time (90 minutes). I used to go home at lunchtime for my grub (and my tickle off Mom), and then belt back to school to preside over these games of football, which were either School Team v The Rest, which could entail eleven against up to 30 kids, or Top Class v The Rest where good players from the school team could be ranged against us.

The boys' playground lent itself to these games as it was rectangular and had two natural goals. One was the previously mentioned boys' outdoor toilet wall, this being the one over which we used to pee on unsuspecting fellow pupils; while the other goal was the wall to the girls' playground, the outside post being demarked by the gateway to the girls' playground so that any off-target piledriver would fly through the gateway and probably take out some poor female who was halfway through 'Tap-a-rap-a rap-a on my shoulder' (boompf!!!). Cue unconscious girl on the floor amid great merriment and/or total disinterest from the boys.

Being a nerd for statistics, I counted all the goals I scored in these games in the final year and set myself a target of 200 goals, which I reached joyously and gloriously with my last ever strike at goal in the final playtime in July 1962, on the day we left the Primary School for ever. I dribbled across the penalty box parallel to the goal, before letting fly with a powerful drive all along the floor which thudded against the wall to my utter glee. I set off on a lap of honour around the playground to celebrate my 200th goal while the rest of the kids wondered what the hell I was doing. It was a foretaste and a replica of many goals scored by Steve Bull 25 years later during his glorious 306 goal rampage for Wolves.

I only missed one game in three seasons for Bearwood Road and that was when my Mom had booked a photoshoot at the local photographer for me to have snaps taken in my Bearwood Road uniform and my choir robes. Despite my protestations to her that a school footie match was way more important than some soppy photos she was unmoved, and refused to change the photographer's appointment. You can tell by the look of defiance on my face and my tightly folded arms in the school uniform photo that I was not happy with the situation.

Living so close to Lightwoods Park with its Extension, (or The Extensh as we called it) and its glorious expanses of grass which were kept cut to 'Football League' standards by Birmingham Parks Department was wonderful.

The Park has never been surpassed in my eyes for its sheer beauty and verdure, and its playing areas lent themselves to the constant participation me and my friends demanded and needed. Us kids from our neighbourhood spent every waking hour playing football there. In the lighter nights we would play there after tea, and at weekends we would be there, although my God-fearing Mom only allowed me out of the house on Sundays to go to Church!

During school holidays we virtually lived in the park. Endless games of attack and defence would take place with my mates Rod Lucas, Mickey and Steve Carroll, Kenny Dearn, Seamus Gillespie, Rob Millward, Alan 'Aggie' Jarvis, Robert 'Oscar' Wilde, Clive Tatton, Chris Millington, Lindsey Grose and various infrequent guest players, until a group of lads who lived a bus ride away in the nearby Birmingham suburb of Winson Green would regularly turn up and challenge us to a game, our lot versus their lot. These games started to take place more and more often and were played seriously and contested fiercely. We never really knew each other's names; it was simply enough that we played against each other flat out.

It was in these games that my skill levels went up a gear as I became fitter, quicker and sharper due to the sheer volume of footie we were involved in. One of the other lot was a lad who had some sort of metal brace on his left leg, and he used to play at the back for them. Whilst he had no discernible speed over the ground, if you allowed yourself to get close enough to him to be tackled, then the force from the contact of his metal-assisted left leg was akin to being hit by a truck. But you couldn't complain because he was disabled. Where was my Dad's safety pin when I needed it!!!!!

As I moved on to Grammar School my addiction to sport had taken hold of me completely, but such was the sharpness of my pre-teen brain that I not only had the academic side of things at my feet through my thirst for general knowledge, but I also spent every minute possible reading the newspapers (from back page to front, of course), watching TV and listening to the wireless, or the radio as we now call it. The eleven-year-old me was a brain at school and had an encyclopaedic knowledge of sport.

Not just football, but cricket, horse racing, tennis, golf, athletics all came under the reach of my brain. It was at this time that I probably stood on the brink of achieving something remarkable with my still young life, but entering the Grammar School, which should have been the portent of a great career at whatever I chose, seemed to herald a spiral into the dissolution of that promise. I was about to start squandering the natural gifts with which I had been blessed.

Chapter Four – Football at the Grammar School

Entering the Grammar School in September 1962 I was, of course, placed in the top stream, the Remove, which was based on my academic achievement in the Eleven Plus exam. There weren't many in that form who could hold a candle to the sharpness or range of my brain, but I had been seduced by stories of my brother and his contemporaries 'playing up' and making the teachers' lives hell. Also, the class would notice me more if I made myself the centre of attention with my 'playing up'.

I did as well as could be expected in the school exams at the end of the first term, but that was the zenith of my achievement, as my behaviour now contributed to a three-year slide in performance, culminating, in true football fashion, to my being relegated from the Remove to the middle stream, the Shell. I only had myself to blame, and I was a constant topic amongst the teaching staff, as they could not understand why such a talented boy could waste his brainpower through stupid behaviour and laziness in class.

Curiously, my football career went the same way. When we started at the Grammar School the sports teachers asked which boys had played for their Primary school teams, and fortunately I was chosen for the squad from which the Under 12 team would be selected. I made the final cut but strangely was selected at left back, a position totally foreign to me but one in which I was to become hugely acquainted in the years to come.

But I only lasted a few games in the team. Two reasons – there were a large number of very talented footballers who hit the ground running at Grammar School, mostly in my favoured position up front, and the other I started to put weight on and lost a lot of the assets which had seen me leave Primary School at the top of my game.

Towards the end of my first year at Grammar School a very distressing and tragic event occurred. Greg Taylor was 17 years old and was in the Lower Sixth. He was the older brother of Peter, one of the gang of three of us (with John and me) who were academically promoted a year at Bearwood Road School. Greg was the star of the Holly Lodge football First XI team. He was the Lodge's equivalent of Duncan Edwards as he was a big, well-proportioned footballer, who could attack and defend with equal skill and he was a genuine Rolls Royce of a player.

One night after school, when I had stayed behind for Under 12 football practice, I found myself in the company of Greg who had been at first XI practice and we started the long walk home. He was very encouraging in what he was saying to me about my football and gave me an insight into playing at the level he was at. I said goodbye to him at about six o'clock outside his home, which we reached before I got to my own home.

The following morning I stood in the school assembly and disbelievingly heard Jim Thorp, the Headmaster, solemnly inform the school that Greg Taylor had passed away during the night, at home in his bed. To this day I cannot come to terms with his passing and feel privileged that I shared that last walk home from school with him. Why was someone so good and so talented taken from us so early? One day we will find out.

Although I was sinking without trace in the classroom, the sheer weight of homework still meant that I was chained to my schoolbooks in the evening instead of playing football and my fitness, I suppose, suffered. Eventually I returned to my mates in the park during the school holidays having been reduced to the ranks as far as school football was concerned. Adjoining Lightwoods Park was another gloriously beautiful park named Warley Woods. The Woods contained a 9 hole Municipal Golf Course which filled half of the acreage whilst the other half was filled with trees and vast expanses of greenery, albeit on steepish slopes.

In the depths of wintertime, one of these slopes would see hundreds of children and adults sledging in the snow on what was known locally as The Death Track. The name arose because legend had it that someone once sledged at speed into a tree and terminated their existence thus giving the slope its name. But the valley formed where the two steep sided slopes met did level out at one point and it was here that I started to play football on Saturday mornings with some of the lads from school, those I might add who were also, like myself, not required by the school team.

During these games my form and fitness gradually started to return and on my fourteenth birthday I had a medical which I duly passed thus enabling me to start a paper round. I delivered my papers by bike, morning and evening, sometimes doing extra rounds for those who were absent.

My trick, which I had inherited from my brother, was to leave the paper shop by bike, deliver all the newspapers without stopping the bike and returning home, all non-stop. This was possible as the houses I was delivering to, in what was the most affluent part of Harborne, all had a dual entrance drive, so I rode in one entrance, threw the papers expertly at the storm porch at no little velocity and rode out of the other side and on to the next house. And I was good at this. The weight I had gained was now falling off me, my speed was returning and I was back to being an extremely talented footballer, and, little did I realise it, I was probably no slouch on a bike either. There were also girls watching us play, and I had not as yet succumbed to this distraction.

It was really a blessing in disguise that I was riding my bike to and from school more often than not as it kept me off the school bus, the X27. The school provided four buses, one was the number two twelve, which took schoolkids back to the depths of Smethwick in the Windmill Lane and Cape Hill areas, and three X27s, which mirrored the 221 bus route from the Kings Head, Bearwood bus terminus to Holly Lane, West Smethwick, where the Grammar School was situated. The X27 bus stop was but fifty paces from my house so this was a doddle for me.

The three buses would arrive in the morning at 8.35, 8.40 and 8.45 and their secondary purpose was to keep us lot, boys and girls, or the Smethwick equivalents of Dotheboys Hall and St Trinian's, away from the apprehensive members of the public using the 221.

In the evening we used to congregate in Forster Street at the side of the Girls' School and when the first bus arrived about two hundred kids would attempt to climb aboard, whilst the despairing conductor stood aside and probably said his rosary. The first X27 would therefore pull away with about one hundred and fifty on board which was way above what Health and Safety legislation would allow today. The second X27 would duly appear some five minutes later and another hundred or so screaming little buggers would shoehorn themselves onto this one. When the coast appeared clear, the third and final X27 would trundle into Forster Street where it would have a more chastened clientele, because these were mostly the kids who had been placed in and served detention for the Smethwick arm of the Hitler Youth, the School prefects.

Jim Thorp, the Boys' Headmaster was constantly reading the Riot Act from the stage during morning assembly to those who frequented the X27 service, due to the repeated reports of intolerable behaviour. One such instance was when a number of us on the upper deck, which was reserved for the boys, but was shared illegally fifty / fifty with the girls, attempted to get into the Guinness Book of World records for the most people you could get on the back seat of a bus. Our numbers were way past what was probably the existing world record when the back window of the bus suddenly dropped out, smashing into smithereens on the pavement below. The record breakers all returned to their original seats at breakneck speed and awaited the thunderous footsteps of the conductor, this time accompanied by the bus driver, who was incandescent with rage.

After he had improved our education by teaching us several new swear words and phrases he duly expelled everyone from his bus and we were all faced with a two mile trudge home, cursing our ill fortune and wondering what delights of punishment would await us when Jim Thorp was appraised of the situation.

I can't remember what he said or did about this particular incident but I recall several of us were expecting at least to be deported to Botany Bay for our trouble. Me and my big mate Rob, two of the protagonists of the above anecdote, still dine out on that one.

My demotion out of the Under 12 school football team meant that I endured a three-year spell in the school team wilderness until the Under 15 year arrived and I embarked on an incredible journey. The season had started with me not even in the school team as usual and ended with me having signed for a Football League Club!

The Under 15 year is the year of the English Schools Trophy, the equivalent of the FA Cup for the representative teams of every borough, town and city in the land. This particular season would end with England hosting the World Cup so football was back at the forefront of everyone's thoughts. Six hundred Schools Associations entered the English Schools Trophy and remarkably Smethwick was the smallest by virtue of it only having 5 senior schools from which the squad was selected. The first round saw Smethwick drawn away to Banbury, with the match being played on the non-league ground of Banbury Spencer FC.

The starting XI contained seven boys from Holly Lodge, and one from each of the other four schools (quota system?). Of the seven Lodge players one was from the year below, the Under 14s, one my big mate Trev Boyle, was from the Remove, and the other five were from my form the Shell. (We reasoned, with some justification, that the Shell was probably the best form team in the country) Banbury were duly despatched 3 goals to 2 so everything seemed rosy in the Smethwick Under 15's garden. Not so, apparently there was a weakness at left back.

Shortly after the Smethwick versus Banbury English Schools trophy match the Lodge Under 15 team, which by association, was pretty strong that season had a practice match arranged at school where they were to be pitted against what was effectively the second choice Under 15 XI, and I was in that reserve team.

What is more, I was to be playing up front. This was the closest I had come to playing for the school team in three years, and in that time I had gone from talented but tubby waster of a player to a resurgent, super slim, super quick and ever-improving talented footballer, all due to my cycling both to school and on my paper round. At least I thought I was a super slim, super quick and ever-improving talented footballer. I took my place on the pitch against this brilliant Under 15 team to await the inevitable hammering. But what happened was probably the most significant football match in which I ever participated. The reserves, which we effectively were, beat the School Team 6 goals to two, and I scored five of them! There was a group of pigeons which suddenly had a cat (me!) put amongst them.

The captain of the School Team, the Town team and also the England Under 15 team was a colossus of a footballer called Lyndon Hughes, who was also in our form, the Shell, and he and the other Smethwick representative players in the school team decided that I was the answer to the Town's problems at left back, so after lobbying the joint managers of the Town team, Dai Thomas and Richard Lear I was drafted into the second round match in the English Schools Trophy, which was away to Stoke-on-Trent, one of the strongest associations in the country. Left back? I didn't have a clue what I was supposed to do, I was going to have to rely on my knowledge of the game and hope that I didn't get taken to the cleaners by some lad who was destined for stardom.

Smethwick won 2 goals to one. All I can remember of the game was that 'Hey, You! Get Offa My Cloud!' by the Rolling Stones was number one at the time in the charts and it was playing on the radio as our coach pulled into the ground. Almost in passing I shared the same name as the Rolling Stones lead guitarist, Brian Jones, although no-one ever seemed to notice or remark on it. I suppose it was a good job my name wasn't Ringo Starr, when I would never have heard the end of it.

Later on when I was 18 and reporting for duty on my summer job at Butlin's Holiday Camp in Minehead with my big mate Trev the day after Jones had been found dead at the bottom of his swimming pool, did someone remark when they saw my name, "Oh didn't you die yesterday?" Clearly not; otherwise I wouldn't have been reporting for duty at Butlin's, now would I?

I was now in the Town Representative team and I hadn't even played for the school team! Life now revolved around midweek training sessions with the representative squad and the local press were starting to take notice as our two away successes had caused a flicker of interest.

The next round saw us drawn at home against Hereford and the match was to be played at Hadley Stadium, Smethwick, just across the road from my big mate Trev's house. The local schools were contacting Rent-a-Crowd to fill the stadium for us. Hadley was a newly built state of the art athletics track which had a football pitch in its centre and a sizeable grandstand running down the length of the nearside touchline, holding about 1500 seated spectators.

I remember reporting for duty in the dressing room on the morning of the game and feeling dead nervous because we could hear the chattering of the crowd arriving and all my mates and my Dad would be there. Mom wouldn't be attending but was content to send me to the game with a bowl of her piping hot porridge inside me. The Smethwick representative side played in an (authentic) discarded Wolves kit of old gold shirts, black shorts and gold and black socks, which pleased me enormously even if it hacked off the rest of team as they were mostly West Brom supporters with the occasional Villa lad thrown in. Hereford were duly dispatched from the Trophy nursing a 6-nil thrashing. The colossus that was Lyndon Hughes scored all six and this now really put us on the map. Lyndon was of course the star, and rightly so; and these three victories now really constituted a Cup run.

The local press started to clamour for their time with us. The Smethwick Telephone, the long-since defunct rag which informed the town's inhabitants of everything happening Smethwick-wise, sent their photographer to do a photoshoot of the team one afternoon at Holly Lodge, where most of us hung out.

He told us that he had a tight schedule and would need to take the picture, note down our names (first name, then surname) and get himself gone. I was sitting second on the front row and the lad on the outside of me was our right back Eamonn Kenna, a brilliantly unruffled full back, unlike the writer! The journo duly snapped the photo then took out his notebook to hurriedly write down our names. He said to Eamonn "you start then, lad" whereupon Eamonn, who had misheard the hurried instructions, replied "Eamonn Kenna". The harassed photographer retorted, "Don't piss me about son, what does the A stand for?" What a belter!

There was a really grounding moment for me during the Hereford game, I was plying my left back trade on the grandstand side when one of our players was fouled and left in a heap injured and requiring treatment. I was deputed to take the free kick on the halfway line and waited with the ball at my feet whilst the trainer did his magic sponge bit.

Our tall defenders ambled upfield to join our strikers in the Hereford box eagerly awaiting my inch perfect delivery for yet another assault on the Hereford goal. The 1500 crowd behind me had a ringside seat as they anticipated my kick. The injury was cleared up and the ref blew his whistle, whereupon I fluffed my lines and scuffed the free kick about ten yards along the ground to the only opposition player occupying the same postcode as me. I searched in vain for the hole that I wanted to appear and swallow me up at that moment.

The fourth round saw us drawn at home to Kings Norton, an association from Birmingham so this was a local derby to savour as the opposition had a proud history in this competition, producing many fine players including the Latchford brothers, Dave, Bob and Peter, all of whom played First Division football, indeed Bob had dozens of England caps earned as a raw-boned, rampaging centre forward. This game was to give me my finest moment in a Smethwick shirt as in front of another big Hadley Stadium crowd, the ball ran towards me on the halfway line and, (as they all say) I spotted the keeper off his line and so I belted it in his direction.

I found the sweet spot on my right boot and watched with delight as the ball cleared the keeper, bouncing once and once only before nestling snugly in the back of the net. Cue pandemonium from my teammates! Yet again we were victorious by 3 goals to one and that evening the Sports Argus, Birmingham's famous football pink paper, produced on the final whistle every Saturday, carried a report of our game, noting that I scored with a speculative shot from about 45 yards. And the rest, Mr Reporter! Oh, and speculative? Not so, it was deliberate!

We were now headline news and we waited eagerly for details of our fifth-round draw. Not good news though as we were drawn away to Newham, from the East End of London, and could expect a tough game as this borough's boundaries contained the mighty West Ham United, an established First Division team, who would presumably be watching this game so they could scout their next intake of apprentice professionals, no doubt.

Amazingly I was now fully involved in the Smethwick Schools Association Representative Under 15 XI's greatest ever Cup run, with little idea of how I had come to be involved but loving this taste of fame as the local press coverage was picking up all the time. My schoolwork as I was now in the Lower Fifths, or the pre-GCE O Level year continued to suffer as my work ethic was hardly improving with this football malarkey taking centre stage.

At least I was doing something positive with my football involvement instead of just idling away my time by acting the fool, being bone idle or just plain daydreaming my schooldays away. As I was in form Lower 5 Shell, at least half of the Smethwick team were my classmates.

And my obsession with sport and almost total reluctance to concentrate in class meant that I was not only dragging myself down, but the other lads too, in all likelihood. We would sit at the back of the classroom and while, for example our History master was droning on (with his eyes shut, usually) about the Unification of Germany and the Chancellor Otto von Bismarck, we would all compete against each other to produce as quickly as possible an ex-Everton team, in the correct positions of course; or a team of players whose surnames began with the letter C. This naturally was immense fun but our parents would have been apoplectic had they known. I think we were all seduced by our glimpse of the big time which this Cup run was providing.

One of our number, the aforementioned Lyndon Hughes knew his immediate career progression. As I have already stated, he was a colossus of a footballer, a man while we were still boys. He had everything - stature, speed (he used to win most of the events in the school athletic sports as well) and the ability to put the ball in the net on a wonderfully regular basis.

He had been training with West Bromwich Albion for some time and, due to the school-leaving age being raised to 16, would have to wait another year until he had taken his O Levels in the Upper Fifths before he could sign professional forms with the First Division club, which he duly did. And with no little success. I recall he made his debut against the Arsenal at the Hawthorns when he was still only 17, and memorably he did for the notorious Scotland and Arsenal hardman central defender Ian Ure in mid-air! All of us, his classmates and teammates, were in the crowd at the Smethwick End, and we cheered this occurrence to the rafters. He made over 100 appearances for WBA in the First Division before moving to Peterborough United.

Lyndon was also captain of the England schoolboys Under 15 team, and when he led them out at Wembley stadium for the Schoolboy International in front of 98000 adoring fans he tells us that he was moved by the crowd chanting 'Lyndon! Lyndon!'. He tells this story against himself because the crowd were actually singing 'England! England!"

Our classroom activities probably reached their nadir with the school Tuck Shop antics which we disgracefully perpetrated on a daily basis. This tuck shop was originally introduced to the school by an ancient English Literature master named Frank Haynes, or Jake as he was lovingly nicknamed around the school. He was a dead ringer for Albert Steptoe and when he left the Lodge he became registrar at the same Cambridge University College which Prince Charles was to study at; and lo and behold, when the TV news footage showed Bonnie Prince Charlie arriving for the first time at Cambridge, who should be welcoming him but none other than Jake Haynes. I have no lipreading skills whatsoever but folklore demands that Charles greeted him with the words "Hallo Jake!" Fame indeed.

Anyway, the tuck shop used to fling wide its portals during morning Short Break between 10.45 and 11 o'clock. Carton after carton of chocolate bars would be transported to the selected classroom where the whole school would queue up like an amorphous blob reminiscent of a football ground emptying to fill their faces with the best that Cadbury's and Rowntree's could provide.

Then Jake decamped to take his road to glory at the University of Cambridge and the tuck shop was taken on by Trevor Howells, a tiny bespectacled Welshman who used to teach History, but had now retrained as a Maths teacher, much to our chagrin. Due to his stature he was known as Erk, but he made up for his lack of inches with a volcanic temper. Quite frequently, during our chaotic Maths lessons, he would launch the wooden board rubber prodigious distances: in your direction if you were the miscreant, not caring who or how many it took out on its missile-like trajectory. That was, if he couldn't smash you about the head with the back of his hand with a force that would have dislodged Nelson's Column from its plinth. What a joy those Maths lessons were.

If our form had Erk for Maths in the period leading up to Short Break, he would terminate the teaching element of the proceedings fifteen minutes early, and take a group of us down to the Staff snooker room where the chocolate cartons were stored; and then march, Pied Piper-like, along the corridor past the other classrooms to the tuck shop classroom, with the choccie-bearing boys trailing in his slipstream. As he passed each classroom, the doors would open and grasping hands would help themselves to free tuck as Erk was oblivious to his rapidly-lessening stock levels. When he was serving it was a well-used tactic to distract him and then get an accomplice to help himself from the cartons, passing back the ill-gotten booty to eagerly-waiting hands in the queue.

Erk also used to leave the cash tin on his desk during our Maths lessons, so that when he decamped to the staff snooker room to get the tuck, we used to help ourselves from this tin to supplement our pocket money. I don't think he ever found out what was going on; which was a good job, because I think the Deputy Head Pop Haley suspected; and if he had had the evidence would have had several of us, and me in particular, roasted on a spit. Like most of the anecdotes in this book I owe Erk, sorry, Mr Howells an apology when next we meet at the great tuck shop in the sky.

I have not met Trevor Boyle over the years as often as I wish I had done; principally because he has lived in Paris for over forty years, but also because I have not made the effort to meet him as often as I should have done. For that I apologise.

But you can never engage Trev in a conversation about Holly Lodge without him mentioning two stories: one about Doc Clark and the other about Laurence McIver.

Doctor Richard Clark was our French master, and he was a brilliantly gifted teacher. Doc Clark would have little sayings which if you learnt them by heart would see you safely through any exam. My own favourite, which had been passed onto me by my brother was Doc Clark's little poem to describe the superlative of best, which was:

'Good, better, best, never let it rest

Until the good is better, and the better best'

This helped with the French words bon, mieux and meilleur (good, better, best). The point of this story is that we used to have French with Doc Clark in the dilapidated classroom next to the Music Room which had a high book cabinet behind the teacher's desk.

When you moved in front of the cupboard the old wooden door creaked slowly open and Doc Clark moved away from the desk and began his 'Good, better, best' routine.

On finishing it he turned to move back to his desk while receiving our rapturous applause, and promptly walked nose first into the cupboard door in a scene straight out of 'Carry On Teacher'. Doc's smooth persona was shattered by this slapstick moment and Trev has retold this story many times, convulsed with laughter. I know you had to be there, but it is worth rehearing it in Trev's company to see the hilarity he found in Doc Clark's misfortune.

The other story centres around the underground passageway which joined the Boys' School to the Girls' School. Heaven only knows how many boys used that secret route into the Girls' School over the years (and for what purpose!!) but we discovered the entrance to the tunnel near to the Staff snooker room downstairs.

To enter the tunnel one had to open a grating which was situated at waist height, and once you had climbed in you had to walk Groucho Marx style, as the head clearance started at about four feet. This clearance gradually decreased as the tunnel reflected the slope on which the school was built. The early part of the tunnel went underneath the quadrangle which was rectangular and had right angled corners. Two problems presented themselves. Firstly, there was very little light; and secondly, the central heating pipes ran across the direction in which one would be Groucho Marxing.

About nine or ten of us made the climb into the tunnel one day, and off we trekked. As we went around the first right angle, there was a loud echoing metallic boinging behind us which we thought no more about at that precise moment.

When we got out the other end, we were one man down in number. By process of elimination someone posed the not unreasonable question "So where's McIver?".

Laurence McIver was a clever lad, a Scouser by birth, small in stature but with a waspish sense of humour.

On this occasion we determined that he had bottled out of this escapade, which could easily have led to expulsion if we were caught. We retraced our steps, and shortly before we reached journey's end we found McIver unconscious and with a severe head wound which had been bleeding profusely. The boinging we had heard had been McIver headbutting one of the central heating pipes in the dark and he had rendered himself immediately unconscious.

We extricated him from the tunnel and had to report his injury as the poor lad was probably going to bleed to death, and we had to make up some cock-and-bull story about how he sustained his injury to keep ourselves out of trouble. As I recall, McIver was off school for about three months with his concussion and what could have been a fractured skull. Trevor loves that story if only for the sheer effrontery of what we did and how we got away with it. This story on its own shows how mixing with me at school was an ill-advised concept. Trevor subsequently succeeded hugely in his business life despite me!

But back to the Cup run, and off we set one early Spring Saturday morning to Newham. Excitement on our coach was tangible as we reached London, a place with which few of us were acquainted. We weren't fortunate enough to play the match at Upton Park, then the historic home of West Ham United, but we played at a stadium very similar to our own Hadley Stadium.

The Newham team were stocked with good players and the game progressed with them imposing themselves on us. They scored, and then we equalised. Game on. We got to the last minute of the first half and Newham had a corner. Eamonn and I, the two full backs took up our customary stations on the two posts but curiously I, as the left back was guarding the right-hand post, which was to prove fortuitous.

As the ball swung over it dropped to our midfield dynamo Stevie Nickless on or near our penalty spot on his favoured sledgehammer of a right foot. Now Steve was one of the greatest players I ever played with. He was a powerhouse of a player, he could tackle, pass and had an eye for goal with a shot which packed a real punch.

He was one of the first names on the team sheet and would be in my all-time favourite team of guys I played with. No question. On this day he met the Newham corner with that right foot and made a heavy and clean connection. Problem was the ball was heading over my head and arrowing at some velocity towards our top right-hand corner. Only the boy who was once the 9-year-old diminutive stand-in Bearwood Road goalkeeper now stood between Smethwick going in for the interval with a potentially damaging 2 goals to one deficit or doing something spectacular to ensure parity. Naturally I elected for the latter and flung myself like a salmon to my right and tipped the ball around the post with my right hand. The save of the season.

Now these days it would have been an instant red card, and I would have been branded a cheat (Reverend Basil – cover your ears!). But this was 1966 and the referee ignored me, thankfully, whilst pointing to the penalty spot. We were still in danger of going behind unless Newham missed the penalty. Newham missed the penalty. I had gone from villain to hero, at least in Smethwick's eyes.

The second half was played out in a tense atmosphere and we escaped with a 2-2 draw and the reward of a replay at Hadley Stadium. I am sure Newham, with their vast resources and array of schools still fancied their chances but we put them away at home by 2 goals to nil. (It may have been 3-1).

In between cup ties our joint managers arranged friendly matches to keep our momentum going. Between the Newham game and our sixth-round tie, where we had been drawn away (again) to Luton Schools we were to play at Coventry City's training ground at Ryton-on-Dunsmore in Warwickshire for a floodlit game against their FA Youth Cup Squad.

In other words, Smethwick Under 15s against Coventry City's Under 18 full-time professional squad. The Sky Blues contained such luminaries as Willie Carr, the diminutive midfield ballplayer who was destined to have a great career with Scotland, Coventry and thankfully Wolves. We were no match for the Sky Blues, of course, as we could have told our joint managers before the kick-off, and we were trounced 8 goals to nil.

To this day I still can't see what benefit this was to us. I didn't see the whole match out as in the second half I turned a 50:50 ball into a 40:60 by virtue of the speed, fitness and professional knowhow of the older Coventry player approaching me and when I finally arrived for the tackle, the ball had gone and he followed through, leaving his calling card (his studs) deep in my thigh. I went down like a deflated Zeppelin and lay on the floor convinced that he had broken my leg and ended my Cup run. I was carried off on a stretcher to the dressing room where it transpired that I had got away with a severe dead leg and was able to walk onto the coach home hobbling, but gratefully unaided.

I had another brief injury scare when playing for the school Under 15 team when I chased a through ball in an away game at Tividale Comprehensive and in a fifty situation their goalkeeper reached the ball before me and drove it against my hand. My outstretched left thumb had a chipped bone in it but I finished the game, which we won eight goals to one, and I managed to notch two of them.

The treatment was not to write for three weeks, and my French master was disappointed when he found out that I was left-handed and couldn't take down his dictation, which did nothing for academic development, but then, what did in those wasted days?

We also had a night's training arranged by our managers at The Hawthorns, the home of WBA, who were supported by most of our team. We were changing in the very nice home dressing room when the Head Groundsman, who was the most senior WBA official present at the ground that evening had decided of his own volition that we were not to be allowed onto the pitch because of the weather (what weather?)

and were only to use the red shale running track surrounding his precious pitch. We were allowed to stand briefly in the penalty area for photographs, but no training was done on the pitch and it was a huge let-down. I never forgave WBA for that, but have a heart, I am a Wolves supporter, aren't I?

The bad weather (what weather?) around at that time caused a postponement of the Luton game which gave me time to recover from my injury and take my place in the team for the rearranged fixture, which was the round of the last sixteen (from 600 starting Associations!). Because of the delay in our match the draw for the quarter finals had already been made, and if we could see off Luton, we had the promise of yet another away tie but against the mighty Leeds, and on their famous Elland Road pitch! Incentive indeed.

We duly arrived at Luton Town's Kenilworth Road ground for this rearranged floodlit game which was now to take place on a midweek evening, thus giving it a great atmosphere. on a ground which had been a First Division venue as recently as 1961. We were shown into the away dressing room which had wood-panelled walls and metal coat hooks screwed into it and basically nothing else. You could imagine what Wolves or Manchester United must have thought of a rubbish dressing room like that. Welcome to Luton Town FC.

Before the crowd arrived, we walked down the tunnel to inspect the pitch, which spread out before us like a vast green sward. I had on my best school shoes, polished to a shine, and my school uniform, as we all did and prepared to walk on to the hallowed turf. Whereupon we sank into very liquid mud which completely submerged my pristine shoes, and we quickly realised the pitch was waterlogged and was actually probably still unfit for play.

Only one stand was open, which spanned the full length of the pitch on the players' tunnel side, and two to three thousand people duly turned up. This, though, was the end of the road for us as Luton defeated us by two goals to nil on a night when Lyndon missed at least three one-on-ones against their goalkeeper.

It just wouldn't go in for us that night, and we trooped off the pitch hugely dejected. To compound matters, our coach got back to Smethwick at about one o'clock in the morning, where we found there had been a heavy snowfall and our waiting fathers picked up their disappointed sons and then set off on another perilous journey to our homes.

The Luton game was also notable for a racially motivated incident involving my other big mate Rob Gilding. Now Rob was a big unit. As genial as they come and hugely popular off the pitch. Every sentence uttered by him would contain a punch line and a chuckle and he was in many ways my partner in crime in the classroom.

He was some player too. He was one of our strikers, very skilful, and deceptively quick for a big lad and a prolific goal scorer. But on the pitch Rob had the shortest of fuses. When we played in the same Sunday league team a few years later I was deputed by our manager to be the one to pull Rob away from any trouble so that he didn't keep getting sent off and suspended.

In the Luton game there was an injury break and Rob and I were on the far side of the field, where the stand hadn't been opened for the game. Except there was one bloke there. To set the scene for this unsavoury incident, Smethwick was going through a period of national notoriety at the time due to a racially aggravated General Election campaign which saw the long-standing Labour Member of Parliament, Patrick Gordon Walker, defeated controversially by the Conservative candidate Peter Griffiths.

The Smethwickian air had been crackling with racial undertones, due to the huge Caribbean and Asian immigrant population newly settled in Smethwick. The town even had a visit from the American racial activist Malcolm X to Marshall Street, where there was an entrance to Holly Lodge Grammar School. This visit was covered in full by national, as well as local television news programmes and all the national press.

This had well and truly put Smethwick on the map. Malcolm X was assassinated back in his homeland some eight days after his visit to Smethwick.

This solitary bloke on the far side of the ground unleashed a foul-mouthed tirade of racial abuse at Rob, besmirching not only the name of our town but us as players (we were 15 years old, for goodness' sake, and he was blaming us for the racial tension in the town).

What he knew about it one hundred miles away in Luton was anybody's guess, but he had picked the wrong man in Rob, who proceeded to march towards him in that manner of his I had seen before which meant he had smelt blood. I actually saved this bloke from the wrath of Rob by getting between Rob's purposeful stomp and this sewer rat before the guy was duly separated from his vital organs. That would have been a tricky one for the referee to sort out. I think the bobbies on duty sorted him out, and ejected him from the ground. Probably dropped him back down the drain from which he had emerged.

Our defeated squad had one more match to play which was against neighbouring West Bromwich Schools. Although it was a friendly it was a local derby with bragging rights at stake and although we had been on a season long rampage around the whole country West Brom still fancied their chances because, apparently, they usually beat Smethwick. We were the away team and I turned up for the game suffering from lumbago, which I thought was reserved only for older people. I could hardly walk, had great difficulty in running and compounded the situation by committing one of football's cardinal sins because I didn't tell the managers I was unfit. Afraid of losing my place in the side.

An interesting take on matters as this was to be our last game together in what had been an historic season. The West Bromwich side were driven forward by their star right winger who I think was called Stevie Williams, and of course, I would be marking him. I did my best to keep him under control as the game unfolded but, as I could only move at the pace of an asthmatic ant carrying heavy shopping uphill into a stiff headwind, to quote Edmund Blackadder, Williams predictably ran riot and despite our forward line putting their Luton nightmare behind them by scoring four goals we were beaten 5 goals to four. As I still didn't let on about my fitness after the game, the only conclusion the managers could have drawn was that I would have to be replaced if there was another game to play after a nightmare display like they had just witnessed from me.

Smethwick is now part of the Metropolitan Borough of Sandwell, which contains many more schools than the five of Smethwick, so our run in the English Schools Trophy can never be replicated. I am therefore proud and privileged to have been part of that squad and list the usual line-up of that historic team:

(The school is Holly Lodge unless stated otherwise)

Goalkeeper; Tony Johnstone

Full backs: Eamonn Kenna, and Brian Jones

Half backs: Steve Nickless, Paul Slingsby and Roger Stote (Smethwick Hall)

Forwards: Trevor Boyle, Rob Gilding, Dave Guest (Sandwell) Lyndon Hughes (captain) and Allan Chatwin (James Watt Tech)

But there was another twist to this incredible season waiting for me. I was to play in a trial match at Walsall FC, then a Third Division side and a good one, constantly in the shake-up for promotion to the Second Division. They played in white shirts with bright red collars, cuffs and numbers, numbered red shorts and white socks with red tops.

I haven't got the first idea how I came to play in this game, I can only think the joint Smethwick managers had a connection with Walsall and I was to play left back as I had for Smethwick. I was in the Walsall team made up entirely of triallists like me, decked out in the first team kit, and we were to play Pelsall Villa, a local non-League side on their own ground. It seemed this unaccustomed position of left back was to be my route to the big time.

I wasn't even thinking of signing for a professional club when I turned up for the trial and the Walsall Manager, Ray Shaw, came into our dressing room before the game to give us individual instructions on how he wanted each of us to approach the proceedings from our relative positions. I recognised him as he had been Birmingham City's trainer when they had reached the FA Cup Final in 1956.

He instructed me at left back to pivot behind the centre half and cover him when the opposition attacked down our right flank, and to push forward when we attacked down our left flank because our right back would pivot and cover me and the centre half in the same manner.

I have vague recollections of the game and I do know I followed Shaw's concise instructions to the letter as this all made sense to me, such a keen student of the game. The result of this game was of course irrelevant and is long forgotten, and I was informed by Walsall's manager in our dressing room at the end of the game that he wanted to sign me, because he liked the way I read the game.

I would be one of the twelve schoolboys Walsall signed each season who would train twice weekly in the evening with the club at its Fellows Park home ground during term time, and then during school holidays in the football season train full time with the professional squad. I would play for the club on Saturday afternoons but my school would have first call on me on Saturday mornings. And I was to be paid travelling expenses for training and a match fee for Saturdays. I told my Dad, who would be racing home from work in Coventry to drive me to Walsall for the 6.30 training sessions that he could have this money for his petrol costs, but he wouldn't take it and he said I could have it all as pocket money.

Naturally, my head was turned by all of this as I decided I needn't renew my efforts academically, as like Lyndon Hughes, I was going to be a professional footballer once I had sat my GCE O Levels. Or so I reasoned.

Chapter Five – Football and my taste of the Big Time

Pre-season training at Walsall commenced at the beginning of August, and, armed with my Football Association registration form denoting that I was indeed a Walsall FC player, I knuckled down to the training regime.

I would like to place on record here that I was not a great trainer, and the lengthy aerobic running sessions we undertook were knackering, even though they got me hideously fit. We would pound the Fellows Park shale track around the pitch and I lapped up the atmosphere of this small, but atmospheric old ground. After the trainers had run the legs off us, or me in particular, we would do some ball work, and the regimented nature of these disciplines exposed some flaws in my technique.

As a left back and a key defender I had to be more efficient with the ball, so I had work to do to succeed. The first team trainer was Arthur Cox, a military sergeant-major type masochist who later became manager of Derby County and Newcastle United. I remember one Saturday afternoon, when the first team was away playing at Grimsby Town, that news came through that his wife had been killed when a tree had fallen on her car after being struck by lightning. I cut him some slack with the sympathy vote after that, although he threw himself back into his work with his usual sadistic methods.

By the time we had returned to school for the start of the O-Level year I had been a 'professional footballer' for several weeks, and had started turning out for Walsall's junior sides. If we played in the Walsall Minor League then we were the aristocrats, and the local teams took great delight in giving us a good kicking by virtue of the kit we were wearing. But we didn't lose many because we were supposed to be the local elite. I was quite a shy boy when I was out of my comfort zone with lads I didn't really know at the football club, and I had to grin and bear it in the cliques which were present in the home dressing room, where jolly japes such as touching Ralgex onto one's testicles as one emerged from the steamy shower room would habitually cause great hilarity. This had the literal effect of being a slow burner as the cream would set your nuts on fire as it took hold. Every one a winner! The other popular ruse was to stand next to someone in the shower and empty a whole bottle of shampoo on their head when they couldn't see because they had soap in their eyes so that the suds could never be dispersed. Laugh? I nearly started.

On the football side there were lads who were pushing for regular places in the reserve side, the final steppingstone to stardom in the first team. Lads like Melvin Ball and Ron Sattersthwaite were young yet grizzled and competitive left backs, who had an intensity to their game that I would do well to learn from.

A team from Birmingham called Brookhill Athletic was taken on by Walsall as a nursery club to provide players to the professional staff. Two players in particular caught my eye, a big but mobile central defender named Allan Forrest who looked a good bet to make progress; but particularly a skilful, flying left winger called Graham Allner, who not only broke into the England Amateur team (it would probably be called the England C team in its modern guise), but also subsequently became an outrageously successful club manager. This particularly with Kidderminster Harriers, whom he led, during his long spell as manager there, into the Football League for their one and only stint at that level. I believe Kiddie dropped a cobble when they let him go.

We were also served in my age group by Phil Parkes, a towering goalkeeper who shared the same name as the Wolves keeper at the time, and who joined Queens Park Rangers and subsequently earned many England caps; also Ray Train, who made hundreds of appearances in the league, principally for Walsall and then Carlisle Untied; and then by various of the five footballing Clarke brothers from Willenhall.

Frank Clarke, the oldest sibling, played most of his professional career for Shrewsbury Town. Then came Allan 'Sniffer' Clarke, who earned dozens of England caps after signing for the all-conquering Leeds United team managed by Don Revie. Sniffer famously headed the only goal of the 1969 FA Cup Final which gave Leeds their first ever trophy success. In between Walsall and Leeds Sniffer was tempted away by Fulham for the princely sum of £100000, and I witnessed this transfer unfold.

It was during the half-term holiday and I was training with the professionals, and was actually taking part in a five-a-side game in the cramped Fellows Park gymnasium between us schoolboys against injured pros who were on the rehab path back from injury. The gym door opened, and there stood the Walsall secretary with two or three men in big hats and big coats, looking like something from "The Untouchables", the popular American gangster TV series at the time. "These gentlemen have come up from Fulham Football Club to talk to you Clarkey, so come on", intoned the club secretary. Within the hour he was gone, signed, sealed and about to be delivered in the big Fulham limo.

The third brother was Derek, who had a spell with Walsall, and then took the journeyman route around the lower divisions. Then there was Kelvin, who unlike his three older brothers, all centre forwards, was a defender, The youngest one, and the second best player after Sniffer, was Wayne, who used to come and have a pre-match kickabout when he was four years old when big brother Derek was in our side. You could see even at that age that he would probably have got in the England Under-Five side and he went on to play with distinction, scoring goals for Wolves, Everton and Birmingham City.

But school loomed on the horizon again and after England's historic World Cup win on July 30th 1966, September beckoned and I re-entered Holly Lodge in the Upper Fifths to commence my GCE O Level year. My footballing mates were astounded that I was now a 'seasoned pro' with Walsall as some of my Smethwick teammates had inexplicably failed to have been noticed by League scouts.

That long and wonderful Cup run had somehow escaped the notice of people whose job it was to pick up new talent, and astonishingly I appeared to have been the only one of that team signed during the long summer holidays, following existing teammates Lyndon (at WBA), Roger (Port Vale) and Allan (Northampton Town) who had all been signed months before.

Two players in particular would have been signed nine times out of ten after trial matches, Stevie Nickless, our dynamic midfield player, and Paul Slingsby, or Slinga, who was a year younger than the rest of the team, but was a staggeringly competitive all-action central defender fearless in the air, brilliantly mobile on the ground, and had a goalscoring presence in the opposition box. I don't think he played for England Schoolboys, which is amazing, as there just could not have been a central defender in the country as talented as he was.

As the FA rules decreed, players signed by League clubs on schoolboy forms had to remain first choice for their schools, which meant in practice that if the school and Walsall had matches which clashed, then school had preference. It never occurred. We were too old for age group football and were now in the realms of First and Second XI squads which meant that if we stayed on for another two years in the Sixth form, then we had three years football ahead of us.

A big surprise awaited us when the School First XI captain came to select the team for the first game of the season, the big local derby against Oldbury Grammar School. Only four players from the Upper Sixth were selected, none from the Lower Sixth, with the other players being the seven of us who had represented Smethwick Under 15s the season before. We were selected for football at Under 18 level when we were fledgling Under 16s.

My meteoric rise was continuing, except that the First XI already had a left back, so where was I selected? Clues were I was 5 feet 9 inches tall, preferred position - striker. You guessed it – centre half!

Where that one came from I haven't a clue, and it was another position I had never played in before, so I was going to have to rely on what I had learnt at Walsall, and fast!

Oldbury Grammar were our local rivals. We all knew each other, and in many cases, we were mates. But on the football pitch, no quarter was asked or given. We were the Beatles to their Beach Boys, as we realised while we listened to their raucous renderings of several surfing anthems emanating from their dressing room before the game.

We trusted our skipper Dave Peniket, who obviously believed in us. He was slenderly built, but a superbly-balanced striker of enormous ability, who rampaged around the opposition penalty area like a lion looking for food. He was with West Bromwich Albion, and led their attack that season in their FA Youth Cup squad. Holly Lodge First and Second XIs played in purple, long sleeved shirts (complete with shirt-tails) with gold V-necks, cuffs and numbers, royal blue and gold socks and either navy blue or white shorts. To pull on the shirt was a great thrill.

The Oldbury Grammar match took place on the second Saturday of term away from home so we hoped that this hurriedly put-together team would not disgrace itself at this level. Eventually we were outgunned mainly due to our youth and although we played well, we succumbed to the harsh score line of five goals to two.

The experiment of playing me at centre half had not paid off. What would the school do, make me play in goal next time? Also, this was the first Saturday of my now regular pattern, where immediately after the game my Dad scooped me up and drove me to Walsall where I played my second game of the day. I wasn't the only player doing the school / Walsall double but two games every Saturday, was going to be hard graft.

I was getting away with it because Walsall kept selecting me. But I didn't know what to expect from the school selectors, when I wandered into the school assembly on the Monday after the Oldbury Grammar match, where we awaited the Headmaster's short verbal report of all the games provided by our sports teacher.

The First XI report for the Head though was prepared by the captain Dave Peniket, and I was gobsmacked when I heard the Head say the First XI lost five two, then read out the names of our goal scorers before adding the rider that Brian Jones had acquitted himself well. Not for the first time I couldn't work out what people could see in my defensive play, still can't in fact. But as soon as I returned to my mates in either Lightwoods Park or Warley Woods, I was again that fleet-footed striker.

Back at Walsall a character had emerged named Derek Woodyatt who was a barnstorming striker himself from West Bromwich Technical School; and once he found out I was from Holly Lodge, dedicated himself to bringing our skipper Dave Peniket down a peg or two. Woodyatt convinced anyone within earshot that he was a better player than Dave (for the record, never in a million years), and how he would prove it when our two schools met, which inevitably they did. I had in the meantime kept Dave informed of Derek's ravings, although I believe anyone inside a ten-mile radius could have heard him! Dave meanwhile kept his counsel by remaining the super-cool individual he was.

Imagine my shock then when the grudge match kicked off. I had been retained at centre half, and so lined up behind our skipper who faced his nemesis Derek across the centre circle at kick off. Their paths shouldn't really have crossed, as they would be attacking opposite penalty boxes most of the time, but out on the touchline near the halfway line they clashed, literally.

I can't remember a tackle sparking things off, but as we all followed the ball away from their particular zone, our eyes were suddenly drawn back to them as they were embroiled in a grappling match, locked together repeatedly right and left hooking each other, until they were separated, I think by my big mate Rob, who probably wanted to have a go at Derek himself! Of course, they were both sent off, but then there was the problem of keeping them apart on the touchline.

When we got back to Walsall for training the following Tuesday night news of Derek's misdemeanour had preceded him, and he received a dreadful dressing down and warning from Arthur Cox & Co. I had to smile quietly to myself.

Towards the end of the Christmas term, which also marked the halfway point of the football season, I was obliged to take the mock GCE exams set by the school, the results of which would determine whether or not I was to be entered for the real GCE exams the following Spring. My school report now contained such gems as "If he spent less time being a comedian and more time working his results would be better" and "he has ability but he is not bothering to exert himself" or the pithy and direct "A thoroughly idle and unreliable boy". And these were the more encouraging comments!!!

I had long since stopped taking my report book home, instead forging my Mom's signature (my Dad's was too difficult) which was supposed to signify that she had read it. Therefore this meant that my parents were oblivious to my academic crisis and downhill spiral, of which I had been the sole architect. I sat ten mock exams.

The GCE pass mark was 45% (Grade 6) so my results were compared to that yardstick. English Language was promising, English Literature not far behind. French also meant I was entered for the real thing, Geography was a borderline decision, but I received the benefit of the considerable doubt. Maths was strangely disappointing for one whose mental arithmetic skills could have blown everyone out of the water. I simply hadn't listened to the theory of the topic, so Algebra and Geometry were a little difficult and then there was Calculus. I didn't understand a single word of it, so even if I had been fed a diet of past exam questions, I would have scored 0% with consummate ease.

Science was a weakness. At Chemistry I could have been dangerous; and Physics, well, I could change the batteries in a torch but that was about it. The most fuss was made about History, where my mock score of 28% impressed no-one, and I was told I would not be entered for GCE.

This gave birth to some sort of panic within me, as it dawned on me that my obsession with sport was going to shop me to my parents who would question why their clever, youngest son had suddenly become a moron: and the future was not as rosy as he himself believed, because "What are you going to do if you don't become a professional footballer?", my Mom kept enquiring.

I pleaded to my History teacher to let me enter. He said no. 28% was nowhere near good enough, and it was my own fault for arsing about continually in his lessons. I pleaded once more and he refused once more. In the end, after I had probably threatened to chain myself to his car, he went to the Headmaster to plead his own case, rather than mine. The Head duly sent for me, and to my astonishment he gave me the chance to prove them all wrong by not only entering History GCE but passing the bloody thing!

A strange set of events then took place. With weeks to go, despite all my football commitments, I got my head down and started to work. I ploughed through Maths past papers provided by my brother; and miraculously, with just two weeks to go before the exam, the penny dropped. Suddenly I understood the subject of Maths, and I could now park that while I worked ever harder on the History syllabus. I learnt it by heart. The Unifications of both Germany and Italy, and the run-up to the First World War. How I did it, God only knows, but I entered those GCE exams as prepared as I could be for someone in the middle stream.

The results arrived, and I had pulled off a staggering achievement. I had achieved a Grade 1 in English Language, the only Grade 1 in the whole School! English Literature was also a pass at grade 4. Similarly, Mathematics, which I had found previously indecipherable until the eleventh hour, weighed in with a grade 4; and French was a grade 5 pass. Chemistry was, as predicted, a failure at grade 8, whilst Geography surprisingly a similar result with a grade 7.

Music contributed with a grade 6, but not after I nearly had convulsions during the exam thanks entirely to my mate Merv Bayliss. The Music syllabus for the exam comprised not only a theory paper, at which I was quite good, owing to my years singing in the church choir at St Mary's, but also a practical demonstration for the examiners.

Because I couldn't actually play a musical instrument, I therefore had to prepare three pieces of choral work which I was to sing (solo) whilst accompanied on the pianoforte by my Music teacher, John Sidebottom, who curiously suddenly started calling himself Siddybatarm. We shortened his surname to Side-arse to save us all from any confusion. Mr Sidebottom (insert your own pronunciation here) had spent the weeks leading up to the exam licking me into shape, so that my newly found basso profundo tones could resonate appropriately for the examiners.

We duly assembled in the Music Room on Examination day for this mini-recital. I performed the first two pieces with little problem and then came my piece de resistance – 'Thus Saith The Lord' from Handel's Messiah. This was a deliberate attempt by my tutor to showcase my singing skills with this wonderful extract from the Messiah, with its long, undulating and tricky runs of notes.

As I cleared my throat and clasped my hands under my heaving bosom, I glanced up only to see my mate Merv gurning, and I really mean pulling funny faces at me through the windows of the Music Room from outside on the quadrangle. I nearly wet myself, and I had the greatest difficulty in keeping a straight face as Mr Sidebottom (use previous pronunciation) hammered away on the Joanna.

Anyway, I must have pleased the examiners because I received two nines and a ten from them, scoring 28 out of thirty marks overall. Merv was delighted with his own efforts to thwart me, and instead of marks out of ten he received a hearty kick up the backside from me; although I have to say I saw the funny side of it, even at the time. Needless to say, Merv went on to have a highly successful career as a solicitor in the City of Worcester.

Which only left History. Would the History master be proved right and I would abjectly fail the exam or would I reward the Head's confidence in me with a grade 6 pass? Can you guess? I passed with a grade (guess again) ONE. As with English Language, the only grade 1 pass in the school, including the whole of the top stream, from which I had been summarily demoted two years previously.

I was awarded two subject prizes for English Language and History, which would be presented to me in front of the whole school at the forthcoming Speech Day, when I would have stuck it to the majority of my subject masters - as if my shortcomings had been their fault! I collected my Leaving certificate and left school with a fistful of GCEs.

One of my two prizes was a Collins English-French dictionary, (one chose one's own books for Speech Day); and I didn't actually go to France for another ten years, so when I came to use it, and I was so proud of it, with its ornate label outlining my achievement stuck inside the front cover, I inadvertently left it at the Palace of Versailles, which left me mortified.

As the new football season of 1967-68 dawned, Walsall FC would have to make the decision to either retain or release the 12 schoolboys they had signed at the end of their one season with the club. It transpired that six boys were retained and offered apprentice professional terms and five were released.

The twelfth player Manager Ray Shaw could not make up his mind about – me. He spoke to my Dad, and offered a compromise. If I went back to school and started the two-year Sixth Form journey towards GCE Advanced Level subjects, then he was prepared to take me on for another season, before making a final judgment at the end of what would be my second season. I thought this was an excellent solution, and after consulting my brother, my Dad shook hands with Ray Shaw and I duly signed on for a second season.

I now had the problem of going back to school and getting into the Sixth Form.

This entailed two interviews, one with the Deputy Head Pop Haley and the second with Head Jim Thorp. I entered Pop Haley's office with trepidation. I should state at this point that Pop despised me, which was just reward for the way I had ridden roughshod over the school for the last five years, only to come up with what could loosely be termed 'the goods' in the O level examinations that summer.

My big mate Trev Boyle had fulfilled his potential with ten O-Level passes, and I envied him because he had the schoolwork / sport balance perfectly under control. I therefore went into Pop's office, and he took one look at who had just walked in and thought to himself "Please don't tell me this buffoon wants to go into the Sixth Form". Sorry to disappoint you Pop, but that buffoon wanted to enter the Sixth Form.

His opening gambit was 'No'. His second was 'Not on your Nelly'. His third was 'Over My Dead Body' and his fourth, and clinching response was 'No', one he had used before. In tennis terminology I had been blown away by four aces. I was reduced to goonish responses such as 'Oh, go on' but Pop was immovable. Then he went to see Jim Thorp while I considered Pop's rather defensive response to my plea to become a Sixth former.

I was duly summoned to Jim Thorp's office. He acknowledged my request and asked me why I wanted to enter the Sixth Form when I had ridden roughshod over his school for the previous five years (!). I explained the deal on the table from Walsall FC. Jim considered this himself in silence for what seemed like an eternity, then he opened one of the drawers in his desk and pulled out a letter.

"I have here a letter" he intoned slowly and deliberately "from a firm of city centre stockbrokers in Birmingham, asking me to send a suitable candidate to them to become a trainee stockbroker". I hadn't a clue what a stockbroker was, so not for the first time in my life I made a poorly informed decision, turning the offer down.

Jim seemed to capitulate at that point, asking me what subjects I wanted to study.

I replied that English and History (my two grade one triumphs and the subjects which had earned me two subject prizes) were logical choices; and also French, because I had loved the fortnight I had spent in Lucerne on the school trip to Switzerland when I was fourteen, which was the only reason I could come up with at that moment. He duly concurred, but not before he had laid down the rather stringent ground rules; that I had to keep my nose clean at all times and there would be no second chances if I reverted to type. As I walked back past Pop Haley's office, he called me back in and said he would watch me like a hawk, and if I sneezed out of turn he would escort me personally to the gates, which I would never darken again! Charming.

I therefore entered the Lower Sixth to commence serious study for my three chosen A Level subjects, with a fourth one added called General Studies which seemed to involve taking out a free student subscription to The Times, reading it for two years and then answering questions on why the world was going down the toilet.

My second season at Walsall had begun in the same pattern as the first, with training on Tuesday and Thursday evenings, then playing a match for Walsall on Saturday afternoon after playing a game for the school First XI in the morning. The Tuesday and Thursday evenings proved difficult because I had homework to get done as I was now a student (as opposed to being merely a schoolboy).

An amazing thing happened at Walsall's first home match of this, the 1967/68 season, which I believe was against Gillingham. It was customary for clubs to publish their retained list in its first programme of the new season. Football still operated the Retain and Transfer system until this was soon to be revolutionised by the forward-thinking Manager of Coventry City, Jimmy Hill, who, while he was still a player with Fulham, was chairman of the Profession Footballers Association, the trade union of footballers.

Players didn't have long contracts in those days, their services were either retained for another season or they were made available for transfer to another club.

Curiously, I had been 'retained' but not on schoolboy forms as in the previous season. I was now registered as an Amateur player, which effectively put me on the same level as the professional players, the difference being that I wasn't paid a salary. More's the pity! So the list of retained professional players had a strange addendum – Amateur players – Brian Jones. I had really made the big time, or so I thought. I foolishly didn't keep that programme, which was strange for someone who had been an avid collector, and I have searched fruitlessly for a copy of it from that day to this.

There was a humbling, if amusing incident one Saturday afternoon after a Walsall Third Division home game. If we in the Junior side finished our game in time to get back to Fellows Park and see the end of the first team game, we would go into the ground through the players' entrance and watch the rest of the game from the tunnel; then dive into the first team dressing room for a cuppa and a biscuit while listening to Ray Shaw and Arthur Cox haranguing the first team whether they had won, drawn or lost.

I think Ray Shaw used to delegate the bollockings to Arthur because his deep booming voice put the fear of God into you, and Ray was an easy going, laconic, avuncular kind of guy. This was the familiar good cop, bad cop routine. Anyway, after one particular match when I had hoovered up the biscuits, I made my way out of the players' entrance where I knew my Dad would be waiting in the car for me. I walked into a melee of young fans and for the first and only time in my life I was asked for my autograph! Feeling important and approximately ten feet tall, I duly obliged and after satisfying every request, I made my way to the car, only to hear a young voice behind me say "Who's he then?" One completely deflated amateur footballer, that's who!

But my ego was shortly to receive another temporary boost. Although I was an Under-17 footballer, injuries meant that Walsall couldn't finalise their team for the Under 18 FA Youth Cup tie away to Oxford United one midweek evening. I was named as part of the squad and would play if one or more players failed last minute fitness tests on arrival at Oxford's Manor Ground in Headington.

I had to obtain permission from school to miss the afternoon's lessons, as I had to meet the Walsall team coach at 3pm outside Bird's Custard factory on Digbeth, Birmingham. Pop Haley surprisingly allowed me to go, as it was probably a relief to him to have me off the premises for the afternoon; and accordingly I duly boarded the coach at the appointed time and place. I sat next to Derek Clarke, the middle of the five Clarke brothers, whose only conversation seemed to involve taking the pee out of me for no other reason than he could be a miserable sod towards me.

We got to Oxford and the fitness tests took place and the players passed them, much to my infuriation / relief. Now if I had been undergoing such a test before an FA Youth Cup tie I would ensure I passed it, even if it meant secreting my wooden crutch down my track suit bottoms to disguise my injury; so disappointingly I was named as twelfth man, which accounted for nothing in those days as substitutes weren't yet allowed. It meant I didn't even get stripped off, so I sat on the bench with Ray Shaw, the Walsall Manager, watching while his Walsall Youth XI, even with our future England goalkeeper Phil Parkes between the sticks, get dumped out of the Cup by three goals to nil.

I would compulsorily have to report any injuries I received to the Walsall training staff, especially if any treatment would be required in order to get me playing again at the first opportunity.

In between studying in Sixth Form and my commitments to the football club I did have a little bit of time to spare and I had actually acquired a girlfriend. On Monday nights we would go and visit her Grandma a couple of miles away at her high-rise flat in the depths of Windmill Lane, Smethwick. If we missed the bus from the Kings Head, we would have to walk it, and one Monday evening we were doing just that after it had recently stopped raining. On the pavement ahead of me was one of those green metal, waste high boxes put there by the telephone or electricity company. I didn't realise that these boxes retained standing water on their tops for quite some time after rain so I thought I would give my girlfriend a glimpse of the agility of her Walsall FC-playing boyfriend by lithely leapfrogging over this obstacle.

I took a jaunty, bouncy run up at the box and placed my hands on top of it at some speed.

Unfortunately, my hands shot forward on the slippery surface and the next thing to hit the edge of the box were my thigh muscles, which tipped me over into a full mid-air somersault, and I landed unceremoniously in an ignominious heap, on my back, spread-eagled over the pavement. Having failed abjectly to impress her, said girlfriend was now convulsed with laughter and couldn't speak during the next fifteen minutes for fear of wetting herself. I tried gingerly to get to my feet but had actually torn both thigh muscles, and the following night my Dad took me to Walsall, where I reported my injuries as per instructions, advising them that they had occurred during a football match, although they couldn't work out how I had got identical injuries on both thighs.

Back at school I embarked on a second year in the school First XI, which had the anomaly of containing no players from the Upper Sixth year above us. One lad from that year named Phil made a few appearances, but otherwise the core of the team were those of us who had formed the backbone of that wonderful Smethwick Under 15 team. We had lost Lyndon Hughes, who had taken up his professional contract with WBA; my big mate Rob Gilding, who had gone off to join Midland Bank; and our goalie Tony 'Rooster' Johnstone, who had taken up smoking on a full time basis and gone in search of a job. Our captain was everyone's favourite player Stevie Nickless, who had been justifiably appointed as our leader, and this a year ahead of his time as well, being a Lower Sixth Former. Steve at last deployed me up front, playing in what I considered was my best position in which I could showcase whatever skills I possessed.

Rob Gilding has been my biggest mate from our schooldays, along with Trevor Boyle. You would always have Rob in the trenches with you, he is a great bloke and even now, just like Trev, loves nothing better than to relive our days at Holly Lodge.

I don't think he can utter a sentence without it having a punchline, and his laughter is infectious.

Like Trev, he was 'adopted' by my Mom, and many was the time when he would come to our house and find it a haven as he tried to sort out his chaotic love teenage love life. My Mom even used to sit down and listen to his (mis)adventures on that subject, and even these days I find his organisation of his matters of the heart from those days comical.

One cricket story about Rob always amuses me. I was playing for Smethwick Cricket Club in a Sunday fixture and Rob had shown up to watch the start of the game. Rob had a passing interest in the club as his Uncle Peter was one of the club's greatest supporters. This particular Sunday it transpired that we were a player short at the start of the game. "My mate Rob is outside, perhaps I can ask him to make up our team" I informed the dressing room, who thought this was a good solution to our problem.

The piece of information that I chose to omit was that Rob had never played a game of club cricket in his life. Still, Rob willingly entered the dressing room and several of us contributed an item of kit so that he looked like a cricketer. The captain duly asked Rob if he was a bowler, and when Rob responded in the negative then the conclusion was that he was a batter. So Rob was asked to bat at number four, which, on reflection, was about seven places too high!

Two wickets fell and came the moment for Rob's triumphal march to the crease, though not before I had reminded him which end of bat to hold. He kept asking me "What the hell do I do now?" as I pushed him out of the dressing room door. If you see the ball, just whack it, was probably the sum total of my advice. To be fair, both he and I thought the situation hilarious.

Rob stomped out to the middle and took guard, saying to the umpire "two legs please" as I had instructed him. The bowler delivered the ball, and I doubt whether Rob saw it, as it thudded into the wicketkeeper's gloves behind him.

Rob turned to look at me in the distant pavilion and I put my thumb up which really meant "@Nice to know you Rob" as I feared the next delivery might kill him.

But in one of those "@Great Moments In Our Time" Rob obviously saw the next ball because he smashed it to the boundary for four glorious runs. I rose to my feet in astonishment at this occurrence and Rob turned to the pavilion, raising his bat as if he had just completed a heroic double-century. I don't think he scored any more runs and his cricket career ended that day, but I know Rob carries that boundary stroke around in his personal sporting portfolio. For one brief moment we were Smethwick players together!

Meanwhile, I plodded on as a left back at Walsall until one day, due to injuries, I found myself selected in a game on the left wing. At last a chance to play up front in a position I preferred, because I loved to play wide on the left, where I could cut inside and get a shot away with my right foot.

Of course, wearing a Walsall kit meant it was open day for the gorilla at full back marking me to try and shorten my life expectancy, but on the one occasion everything fell into place I cut inside him and headed for goal, and when I was about six yards out in front of the near post I let fly only to see the ball cannon back off the post, shooting back over my right shoulder and away to safety. Oh well, at least I had shown them I could be a danger man in front of goal, even if my one and only chance to get on the scoresheet for Walsall had gone.

I reached the dressing room after the final whistle expecting a consoling "Hard luck son" from the team manager, only to be informed that good strikers don't panic in front of goal because they find the target on a consistent basis. After that experience I undertook a warm-up ritual before any school game where I was playing as a striker, in that I would smash the ball into the roof of an admittedly empty net time after time, to sharpen me up, so that if there was a ghost of a chance in the six yard box, then I was going to smash it and not 'baby' it.

This ritual had an unfortunate consequence in that before one First XI game I was undergoing my smash-it-in routine when our new goalie, Nigel Howl, Big Nige, thought it was part of his own warm-up to try and stop these nuclear missiles I was firing from within the six yard box. I duly connected with a piledriver from about three yards which hit him on the hand and broke his thumb. I think he played on for the whole of that game, because he wasn't going to let my stupidity stop him playing despite my successful attempt to maim him.

Another goalie failed to get beyond the kick-off in an important game sometime later. This incident occurred in the Upper Sixth when I was captain of the First XI. Big Nige was unavailable and the Second XI goalie was away from school sick on the day of the game. We were playing Greenmore College at home on a Wednesday afternoon in a Birmingham Grammar Schools Cup tie. To fill this emergency goalkeeping vacancy, I could only think of a mate of ours called Jan Kuczerawy, who was tall, but was very definitely an outfield player, albeit a good one in our Second XI. I was sure I had seen him perform adequately in goal during a kickabout so I asked him to help us out of a predicament in between the sticks for that afternoon's Cup tie.

"But….," He started to sa,y and I expected some modesty followed by an acceptance to play; but every time I gave him a chance to speak he kept saying "But….," I was having none of it, so he lined up in goal at my request and I prepared at centre forward to kick off. I then had the bright idea of giving Jan an early touch by sweeping the ball back to him straight from the kick-off. The ball reached Jan who seemed not to know whether to pick it up or stop it with his foot. He started to bend down with all the agility of a rusty crane, but failed miserably to impede the ball's progress as it rolled past him and nestled snugly in the back of our net!

Well, ever the one for statistics, I had probably scored the world's fastest own goal, but more crucially, I ran towards him demanding an explanation, which he duly provided. "You wouldn't let me tell you when you asked me to play, but I have done me groin in and I can't really move".

My fault. As Captain, I had to think quickly.

After 5 seconds play, we were a goal down, and a player down as substitutes had not yet been introduced. There were 89 minutes and 55 seconds left to play. I did the only thing I could think of. I went in goal myself, and I would like to say I produced a heroic display in goal. I didn't. We drew four all. We turned up for the replay with a full complement of players, including the return of Big Nige in goal, but we still got gubbed and exited the competition.

The season progressed at Walsall and at school. Led by the fearless Stevie we had acquitted ourselves well in what was effectively a year ahead of our time; so the portents for the following campaign were good, except that we lost our leader Stevie who didn't stay on for the Upper Sixth, taking up an offer to train to be a Legal Executive with a firm of local solicitors.

It was also decision time for the second time at Walsall FC, which I awaited nervously.

Chapter Six – Football and the End of the Big Time

Walsall Football Club, or Ray Shaw in particular, decided that he had not seen enough from me to enable him to offer me a professional contract, so after two seasons, I was released. Before I had time to feel sorry for myself Stan Howard, the Manager of the Sunday team I was playing for, Tupelo FC, (so-called presumably because Stan, was an Elvis fan and Tupelo, Mississippi, was where Elvis was born) must have had a contact at Shrewsbury Town FC, who played in Division Three in direct opposition to Walsall, and he took me and two other teammates to Shrewsbury to play in a trial match.

I was placed in the attacking midfield role I was currently occupying for Tupelo (!). I played in just about every position on the field for Tupelo so for once I knew what I was doing. I remember in this game storming through the midfield and hitting a rocket which screamed into the top corner from outside the penalty area. I was, quite unbelievably, told I was going to be signed up after the game, and an appointment was made for me to sign in front of the Manager, Harry Gregg.

Harry was a big star and a hero. He was the Manchester United goalkeeper at the time of the Munich Air Crash, which he survived and he had distinguished himself by repeatedly and heroically going back into the burning wreckage extricating survivors. When he passed away as I was writing this book the radio was broadcasting tributes to this wonderful man all day.

He was also the goalkeeper in the 1958 Cup Final only three months after the disaster when the reincarnated Busby Babes lost 2 goals to nil to Bolton Wanderers with the second goal famously allowed when Bolton's Lion of Vienna, Nat Lofthouse shoulder charged Harry Gregg and the ball into the back of the net, knocking Harry unconscious.

These days if you say 'Boo' to a goalkeeper the referee comes over all officious and disallows those goals.

I entered his cramped office and met this famous man and was greeted with a handshake which nearly pulled my arm out of its socket. He was a big, bluff Northern Irishman, with an accent you could saw timber with, he had enormous shoulders and a barrel chest. He didn't smile much either. He hadn't seen me play but was signing me on the recommendation of the coaches who had reported back from the trial game. He looked me up and down and said that I would have to look after myself as he thought I would run to fat as I got older. Charming! But I signed and Shrewsbury Town took the place in my diary of Walsall.

That Tupelo team was an amalgam of half of our lot from Holly Lodge and half of the Oldbury Grammar lot, which was how we knew each other so well. The other half of our lot and the other half of their lot played for another team called Lodge Vale, but the two teams' paths never crossed as we played in different leagues on Sundays. Tupelo played in tangerine coloured shirts with white collars and cuffs with white shorts and tangerine socks. A replica of Blackpool FC's strip. Don't ask me why, I think Stan must have acquired them as a job lot in a sale!

We began as an Under 16 team, and I think it was during our fourth season together that we lost a league game for the first time, as we went through the age group divisions with little difficulty until we found ourselves in the adult North Birmingham Sunday Premier League. We were doing well until we came up against the league leaders Thurlstone United, who seemed to be a bunch of beer-swilling teddy boys. They had been waiting for us and they took us to the cleaners by four goals to one.

Our manager Stan, used to ask me to keep my big mate Rob Gilding out of trouble on the field, and many was the time I had to pull him away from situations, which wasn't as easy as it sounded because he was a big unit and when he smelt blood, a little squirt like me wasn't going to impede his progress towards trouble. Tupelo also played in a winter indoor five-a-side league at Thimblemill Swimming Baths; and our great rivals in this league were Smethwick Hall, who consisted of a couple of gifted players, together with any available thugs to make up their numbers.

One night, in the middle of a keenly contested game, one of the Smethwick Hall desperados attempted (how stupid can you get?) to put Rob over the waste high boards which formed the boundaries of the five-a-side court. Naturally all hell broke loose, and Rob and the would-be assassin were involved in a stand and deliver roundhouse slugging match. Curious as Rob, the afore-mentioned big unit, was confronted by a skinny kid called Brian who was beginning to realise the error of his ways in trying to put Rob over the boards. A mismatch didn't enter into it. Of course, both were sent off and banished to the swimming cubicles which acted as our individual changing rooms.

The game had several minutes left before it reached the final whistle and then we all rushed to the cubicles where Rob was hanging over the top of said Brian's cubicle trying to hammer seven bells out of him after he had locked his cubicle door, preventing Rob's unwelcome entry through the appropriate channel. Rob had a beautiful golden retriever named Triffon, on whom he doted; and I often thought Triff would have been well employed retrieving the situations his master kept getting himself into, as he would have had far more clout than me! Rob, incidentally, off the field is one of the most genial, and genuinely funny people I have ever met. On the field he just lived for the balloon to go up. In the Wild West he would have been legendary!

After Stevie Nickless left school, I was appointed Captain of the First XI and duly installed myself at centre forward, resisting the claims of a lad named Pete Whitby, a year younger than me but who thought he should be the number 9. I disagreed, using my casting vote as captain, and inadvertently gave him a taste of my own medicine by placing him at right back, where he went on to perform superbly all season!

We had a good school team, the nucleus of which had already been together basically for three seasons, and we started to win matches on a frequent basis. I was notching a good number of goals and was to go on and score 23 in that final school season, helped in no small measure by the skilful promptings of my big mate Trev Boyle, who was deployed wide right, but these days would probably be in central midfield where his intelligent passing and prompting would unlock defences from more threatening positions.

Ever the extrovert I had long since started embellishing my Holly Lodge First XI shirt with my gold Wolves shorts, and the familiar Wolves gold socks with two black hoops at the top. They were the ideal complement to the purple and gold First XI shirts. Nobody said I couldn't, so I wore them. I thought it looked brilliant. I did, of course, have the Wolves round necked, long sleeved shirt as well and I wore the full kit at school in practice sessions whenever possible. Again, nobody said I couldn't, so I did.

We all look like someone else in this world I suppose, and I bore a passing resemblance in my full Wolves kit to the rising Wolves superstar Peter Knowles, who was to turn his back on the game in 1969 at the age of 23 to become a Jehovah's Witness. He played his pre-announced final game before retirement against Nottingham Forest at Molineux in September 1969. So earth-shattering was Knowles' sudden departure from the game that BBC Grandstand showed live pictures at the final whistle of him attempting to leave the field of play with the minimum of fuss but being mobbed by his adoring Wolves fanbase.

My Dad said he would not watch the Wolves again unless Peter Knowles returned to play, which he never did. Knowles never played again and my Dad died ten months later. Peter Knowles will remain to my dying day my favourite all-time Wolves player. What a talent he had. However, I would never attempt to make him or anyone renounce their religious beliefs. That is beyond my powers, and rightly so.

My resemblance to Peter Knowles led to a strange incident in our local newsagent when I went in there one day dressed in full Wolves kit to buy a football magazine. Knowles' picture was adorning the front cover of that issue, and the ladies behind the counter executed a classic double take when they saw me and were convinced I was him! Quite humorously they wouldn't believe me, and they insisted I sign a copy of the magazine with an autograph so I scrawled 'Peter Knowles' across the photo and beat a hasty retreat from that madhouse. I think I still had to pay for another, unsullied copy of the magazine! I did say I was only asked for my autograph once, which was at Walsall, I didn't say I hadn't been asked for someone else's!

There were some notable games. We had, in recent seasons, a poor record against our major rivals and friends Oldbury Grammar, who seemed to mesmerise us every time with their silky football. One of the problems had been that they played lads of the right age in their team, where most of us had been playing two and then one year ahead of our time. But one memorable freezing, foggy Saturday morning in January everything came together, and we finally defeated them four goals to two. We dominated the match from the first whistle because they scored their two goals in the last two minutes of the game. We all felt like we were flying after that result!

Smethwick, which was originally in Staffordshire, had now been merged into the newly created borough of Warley, which was placed in Worcestershire during the rearrangement of the county boundaries (totally unnecessary in my view). We played that 1968-69 season therefore in the Worcestershire Schools County Cup, and we found ourselves opposing Bromsgrove Grammar School in the final, which was to take place on our school pitch.

It was in this game that I nearly burnt my boats. It was a frosty morning and the pitch was rock hard. I was being marked, literally, by their monster of a centre half, and when he went through me from behind for the umpteenth time and I landed, stomach first on top of the ball, my sorely tested patience finally snapped.

The free kick was duly awarded, but I pulled the ball from underneath my torso, turned and drop-kicked the ball in the general direction of the retreating monster. As luck, or more accurately, Fate would have it, the ball, struck sweetly by me with some velocity, arrowed like a laser onto the back of said monster's head, laying him out like he had been shot. I rather foolishly accompanied this blockbuster with the words "You do that again and I'll f***ing kill you!" which was, in retrospect, probably an empty threat.

The referee, who was our Sports master, Roger Skelhorn (this was a Cup Final for goodness sake, although a neutral referee would have reached the same conclusion) looked quite shocked as he came over to me and almost apologetically said "I'm sorry, Brian, but I am going to have to send you off for that". I started the very long walk to the dressing room in tears, knowing that I had not only let myself, my Dad (who was on the touchline), my teammates and the school down, but also I would probably be suspended indefinitely from playing for the school team again when the Head Master found out about this. Pop Haley would probably hold a champagne reception by way of celebration!

Our senior Sports Master, Eric Quance, was also on the touchline, standing in close proximity to my Dad, and Eric made some quite justified remarks about my petulance which, I am told, prompted my Dad to lamp him one. Eric then made it a double family sending-off by banishing Dad from the touchline, but Dad stood outside the railings, which meant he was still only two yards from the touchline as the railings and the touchline ran parallel and extremely close to the pavement.

I received an amazing reprieve when the incident, to my disbelief, was not mentioned in the Headmaster's ghosted report of the game at Monday assembly. We had drawn 3 all, and a replay loomed at Bromsgrove's school. I was summoned to Eric's office in the gym and with Roger Skelhorn in attendance, and full credit to them, they both spoke to me like a man.

They told me that they knew what the Headmaster would have done to me had he been furnished with the facts, and they felt I didn't deserve that, and that the sending off was sufficient punishment. They said it was out of character and they knew there would be no repetition. What a wonderful way to defuse a tricky situation. I thanked them for their thoughtfulness, and gave them my own assurance there would be no repeat. I retained the captaincy, we won the replay, and we were crowned Champions of Worcestershire.

This episode was not symptomatic of the callous disregard I usually exhibited for the authority of the teaching staff, although I was grateful, if not pleasantly surprised, to find that Eric Quance and Roger Skelhorn had spoken to me mano a mano.

There was one master, however, who was liked and respected by all of us at Holly Lodge, particularly by me, and that was one of the History Masters, Bill Lewis. Bill was a young Welshman, probably in his early to mid-thirties, and he earned our respect by treating us Sixth Formers as men and equals. He would drink with us at the trendy hostelry that Holly Lodge students, male and female, used, the Chalet in Bearwood, and for the first time we were allowed to call a teacher by his Christian name, and it felt comfortable and natural. Bill used to board the school bus, the X27, on Lightwoods Hill, opposite Warley Woods, where he lived, and muck in with the rest of us. He wore glasses, but was one of the first people I had met who used contact lenses.

Bill was a good athlete, a cross country runner and ran to and from school frequently. He also showed a great interest in the development of the best runner ever produced at the Lodge, Bernard 'Bud' Baldaro, and used to run with Bud around the school grounds. Bud broke the school cross country record, and I wouldn't be at all surprised if his time was never surpassed, he was that good. He became an internationally renowned long-distance coach and a respected columnist in the Athletics world.

And Bill was the number one fan of our First XI football team, home or away. His easy charm was always to be found on the touchline as his South Walian accent could be heard, cajoling and encouraging us but never with a harsh tone in his voice.

One episode endeared me to him, and it was so typical of the way he engaged with us and cared. I had pulled up after one Wednesday school game with a knock after a bruising encounter, and I had limped home fearing that I might not make it for the important match following less than three days later on the Saturday morning. I went to the Chalet with the gang that night, and when I got home on our doorstep I found a brown paper bag. I opened it and inside was a box of Radox Bath Salts, which would help the recovery of aching and damaged muscles. Attached to the box was a note which simply said 'Bill'.

Only twelve months after we left school, we heard that Bill had been diagnosed with cancer, and within weeks he had gone to a better place, tragically young. I will always remember Bill Lewis as one of the nicest and kindest of men, and I am certain my contemporaries will endorse that. I am proud to have known him and thank him for the interest he showed in me. Rest in peace, Bill.

Back to the football, and all of the County Champions were then entered into a nationwide knockout Cup and Holly Lodge, as Champions of Worcestershire, were drawn away to the Champions of Staffordshire, Darlaston Grammar.

A match of some importance deserved a better venue than that provided by Darlaston for the occasion, but we duly despatched them by the odd goal in three on a pitch that one wouldn't have grazed cattle on. We were off on another national Cup run and memories were stirred as we were drawn at home to Ellesmere Port from the Wirral in the next round.

The school booked Hadley Stadium for the big cup tie and the Headmaster gave the whole of the school the afternoon off so they could fill the Stadium and roar us on to victory.

Fig.1 Mom (aged 17) with her Mom, Grandma

Horobin, at Auntie Cis's wedding 1934

Fig.2 Mom and Dad on their wedding day, September 28 1940

Fig. 3 TOP Warley Woods Home Guard Platoon 1940. Dad, extreme left, back row

BOTTOM Author (left) aged 17 with Dad (right) aged 53 in 1968

Fig.4 Author (aged 3) with brother Roger (aged 9)

Fig. 5 TOP First known picture of Author playing football (aged 18 months)

BOTTOM LEFT Rod Lucas, Author (aged 11), Steve Carroll in Lightwoods Park

BOTTOM RIGHT Bearwood Road Football team 1959-60: Author (aged 9) 2nd right front row

Fig.6 TOP First known picture of Author (aged 8) playing cricket with brother Roger batting

BOTTOM Choirboys outing Llandudno 1959, Author (aged 8) riding 2nd donkey from left

Fig.7 Bearwood Road Football team 1959-60

BEHIND Mr Arthur and Mr Jones (Headmaster)

BACK ROW Gordon Blackwell, David Hunt, Bryan Stock, Author (aged 9), Nigel Beer, Kevin Jordan, Johnny Beddall

FRONT ROW Robbie Withers, Alan Dimmick, Andy Fowler, Barry Hitchman, Phil Junkin, Peter Jones.

Fig.8 Bearwood Road Football team 1961-62.

Back row: Chris Teasdale, Michael Bowser, Robert Turner, Robert Millward, Robert Clarke, Jeremy Horton

Front row: Lindsay Grose, Author (aged 11), Kenny Dearn, AN Other

Fig.9 St Mary's Church Choir 1959 – Back row: Mr Sandell (Verger), Ken Sandell, Ian Sandell, Neville Legg, Philip Daniels, Roger Jones, Miles Dunn, Christopher Manning, Roy Dursley, Gordon Dursley, Robert Legg. 2nd Row: Trevor Smith, David Halford, Ron Middleton, Albert Wright, Mr Southall, David Dunn, David Pearson, Barry Wainwight, David Weekes. 3rd Row: AN Other, Mrs Pearson, Mrs Wright, Mr Richard Dunn (Choirmaster), Neville Wright, Revd Basil B F Westcott, Mr Austral Ryley, David Browning, Miss Edna Andrews, Miss Allinson, Verity Butler. Front Row: Nigel Beer, Michael Baines, Author (aged 8), Jimmy Bodfish, Michael Southall, Allan Warren, Craig Burney, Robert Wilde, David McGeever.

Fig.10 Author (aged 11) in St Mary's Choir robes - this picture was taken on the same day as the cover photo

Fig.11 Bearwood Road School Leavers July 1962

Back row:

*Malcolm Frost, Roy Huckfield, Judith Freer, Miss Andrews (Headmistress), Jennifer Parry, Beryl Wood
Jayne Hammond, Jackie Barron, Josephine Junkin, Susan Malbon, Elizabeth James, Janice Wood,
Sarah Deary, Miss Pretty (Class teacher), Mervyn Bayliss, Richard Hill, Clive Parkes*

Front row:

*Andrew Wildman, Jeremy Horton, Lyndsey Humphreys, Sally Smith, Belita Noble, Gillian Beddall,
Mary Tatton, Anne Bridgewater, Linda Geer, Mary Bodfish (who wrote the Foreword to this book),
Anne Young, Graham Stokes, Stephen Morris, Robert Clarke, Robert Millward, Stephen Gough*

*Absent: Author!, Paul Surman, Barbara Mynott, Susan Laurence, Robert Turner, Geoffrey Duckhouse,
Ronald Fieldhouse, Elaine Purshouse*

Fig.13 Holly Lodge Form 4 Remove 1964-65. Back Row: Jeff Baker, Stanislaus Dobrzanski, Paul Surman, Laurence Parkes, Andrew Wildman, Robin Stockley, Lee Taylor, Jeremy Horton, Jan Konstanty, Malcolm Frost, Author (aged 14), Martin Saunders. Middle Row: Christopher Savage, David Mackay, Robert Clarke, Laurence McIver, Malcolm Bailey, Philip Knight, Robert Baker, Trevor Hall, David Benfield, Robert Millward, Trevor Boyle, Graham Flint, Matthew Turley. Front Row: Alan Brown, Nicholas Brimble, Nigel Jackson, Neil Simmonds, Mr Derek Backhouse (Form Master), Graham Cresswell, Andrew Pigott, Stephen Morris, Michael Phipps.

Holly Lodge Under 13 Cricket team 1964. Back row: Mr Boyle (Trevor's Dad),Steve Carroll, Paul Charles, Paul Slingsby, Author (aged 13), Dave Mackay, Pete Furnival. Front Row: Keith Johnson, Nigel Howl, Trevor Boyle, John Llewellyn, Philip Charles.

Fig.13 Holly Lodge First XI Cricket 1965.

Back Row: Micky Phillips, Rod Hancox, AN Other, Roger Pemberton.

Front Row: Andy Phipps, Pete Ashford, Stuart Daly, Mr Bill (Jesse) James, Steve Harvett, Kevin Jordan, Author (aged 14).

Fig.14 Holly Lodge Under 15 Football team 1965-66

Back row: Eamon Kenna, Chris Bedford, Tony Johnstone, Rob Gilding, Author (aged 15), Trevor Boyle, Mr Eric Quince.

Front row: Colin Warren, Kevin Holder, Lyndon Hughes, Paul Slingsby, Steve Nickless.

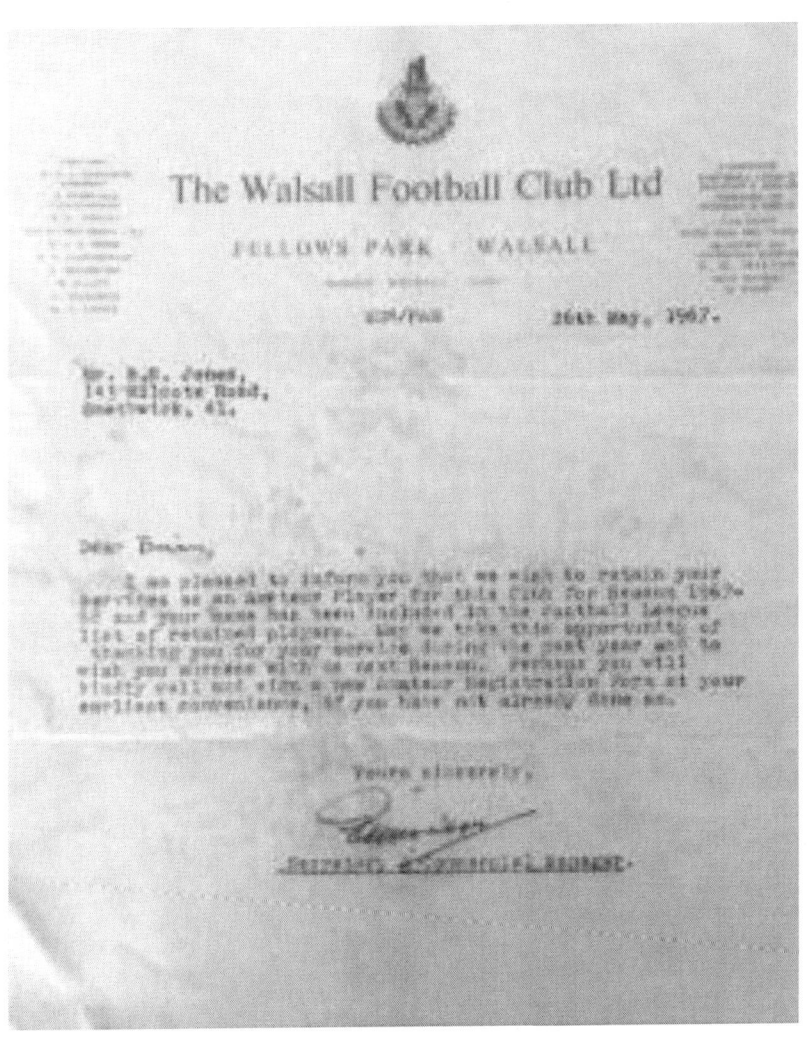

Fig.15 Letter from Walsall Football Club dated 26.05.67 keeping the author on the books for a second season.

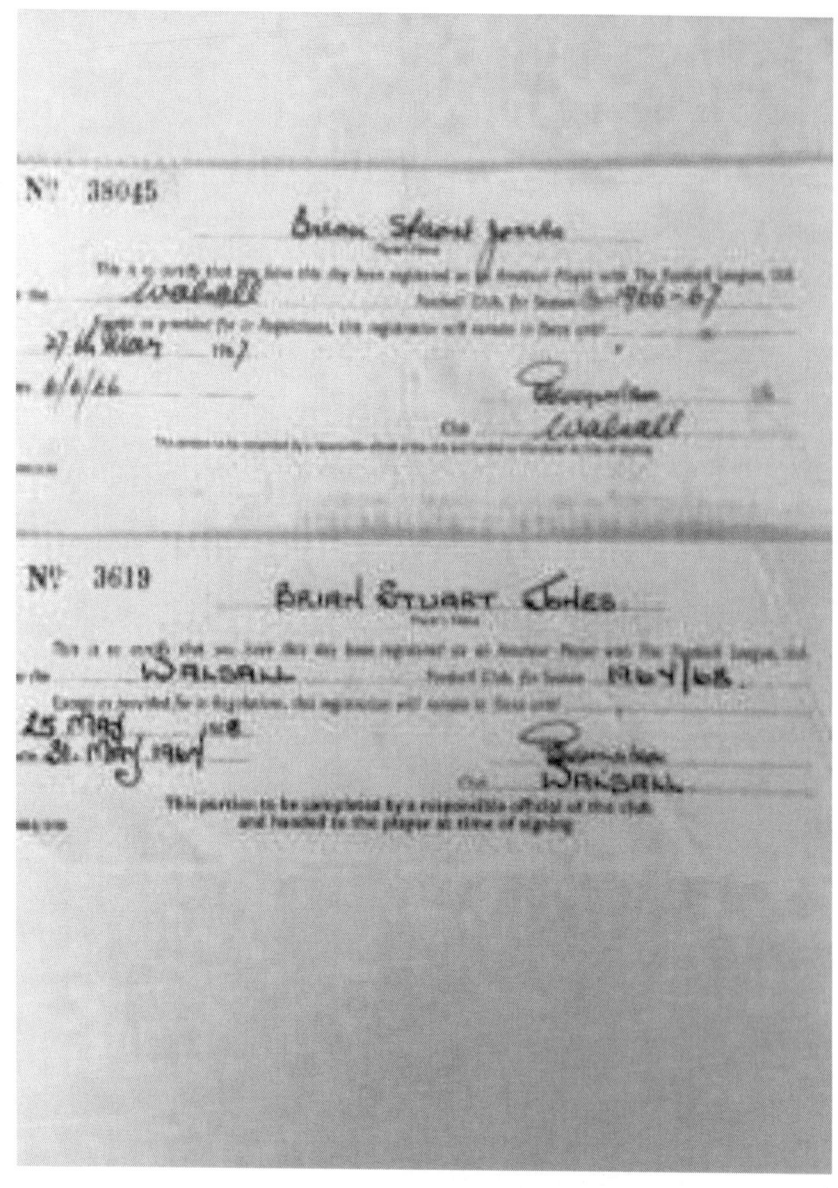

Fig.16 My Football League |registrations for the two seasons with Walsall FC (1966-67 and 67-68)

Fig.17 Holly Lodge Upper Sixth Arts 1968-69

Back Row: Jan Kuczerawy, Roy Lawrence, Eddie Kuczerawy, Steve Nickless.

Front Row: Author (aged 18), Craig Barney, Trevor Boyle, Mr Derek Backhouse, Mervyn Bayliss, Eamon Kenna, Malcolm Bailey.

Fig.18 Tupelo FC circa 1969

Back row: Mr Stan Howard Senior (Manager), Chris Cooper, Stan Howard junior, Billy Atkins, Johnny Stokes, Roy Hodgkinson, Pete Stevenson, Author (aged 19), Mr Tony Dandy (Coach).

Front Row: Tommy Fellows, Colin ?, Johnny Walker, Paul Arnold, Steve Venross.

My big mate Trev Boyle told me recently that John Richards was in the Ellesmere Port line up that day. Richards scored 194 goals for Wolves in the years to come, and to this day stands second only to Steve Bull in the all-time Wolves goalscoring charts. Back to the game, and disappointingly Ellesmere Port gradually wore us down and with five minutes to go were comfortably two goals ahead. Trev then put one on a plate for me, but this goal did not herald a grandstand finish, and we lost, thus bringing down the curtain on a school football career which had begun ten years earlier at Bearwood Road School.

I still have dreams even now of that school team at Holly Lodge. Playing on the top pitch at home on a chilly Saturday morning, with the light brown ball we always used to play with. A ball that would stay hit once you met it correctly, a ball that you could sweep out to the wing and await its return. I dream of big Nige catching a cross and feeding Eamonn, or Slinga or Coggers winning a tackle, and feeding Stevie in the midfield, who would run through a brick wall, and let Trev have it on the wing with a beautifully crafted pass.

Then Trev looking up, and spotting my run, where I would meet his through ball and sweep it past the keeper into the net at the School Drive end. I would watch in awe as Slinga would meet a corner full on and rocket a header into the opposition net, or Stevie would get the ball out from under his feet and hit the net from 25 yards. I still dream about that team. As long as I live and breathe those boys will continue to play football of ethereal quality. No-one has jurisdiction over my dreams.

I want to pay my tribute to the lads in that team by printing the usual (and to me legendary) line-up:

Goalkeeper: Nigel Howl

Full backs: Pete Whitby and Eamonn Kenna

Half backs: Andy Coghill, Paul Slingsby and Steve Nickless

Forwards: Dave Lawley, Trevor Boyle, Brian Jones, Colin Warren and Allan Chatwin

And in the final season Micky Phipps came in at full back for Eamonn Kenna who moved up to replace the school leaver Steve Nickless

What a cracking bunch of players!

My short and completely uneventful career with Shrewsbury Town had come to an abrupt end shortly after Christmas that season. Saturdays now consisted of me playing for the school in a 10 a.m. kick off, then, being driven to Smethwick's Rolfe Street Station to catch the Shrewsbury train which would arrive at about 1.15. If I was playing in an away match then I was bundled into a taxi, at the Shrews' expense, and driven to somewhere light years away, as we would probably be playing in some league in North Wales. I would then get back to Shrewsbury for the return train journey, reaching Smethwick Rolfe Street to be collected by Dad and deposited back home by 9 p.m.

It was a twelve-hour day and it was killing me. I had no enthusiasm for Shrewsbury Town, and after discussing it with my Dad, decided that by pulling out of Shrewsbury it was the end to any pretention I had of being a professional footballer. I did say I have made some ill-advised decisions over time but this one I think was sensible. What it did mean was that my A Level studies, which I had neglected through prioritising football, now had to take centre stage if I was to have any chance of passing them and getting a decent job. I complicated matters as well by playing one of the leading roles in the school play, 'Arms and The Man' by George Bernard Shaw, which became yet another uncalled-for distraction.

In this play I took the role of Major Petkoff, a senior official in the Russian army, and a man of at least sixty summers. Each night my Beatle hairstyle would be doused liberally with talcum powder in order to make me look like an elderly gentleman. After the last night of the play, the Saturday night, we all raced round to my mate Merv's house for the obligatory end of play all night party without bothering to remove make-up (or talcum powder). The following morning I was playing for Tupelo in an Under 18 Cup Final and I duly took up my place at the kick-off replete with grey hair.

The referee, who thought I was way over the age limit, listened long and hard to my unlikely story of the school play and Major Petkoff, but in the end he had to relent and consent to my participation!

But for my A Levels it was too late. I could get by in English Literature, because I could write and speak sufficiently well in exam conditions if I had some idea of the topic in hand, and could understand the syntax of grammar, so it became a question of reading and studying novels, plays and poetry, which was good fun.

French, I neglected badly, because to be fluent in any language one should use it frequently. The French syllabus was complicated further by its literature element, which meant reading French novels and plays. It wasn't enough to try and translate them word for word, because that would take ages, nor was it prudent to read the English translations and try and memorise direct quotations from these works in readiness for the exam. So I was totally unprepared for this upcoming A level torture.

I passed English Literature with a Grade D. Grade E was a pass and Grade F a fail. I predictably failed French. That left History, the cause of all my angst at O Level. I drifted in and out of the syllabus, occasionally producing essays which gained an A from my tutor, but more often than not failing to research exhaustively enough and submitting substandard work. At the eleventh hour I set about memorising the syllabus to try and replicate what I had done for O Level but it was no good. I failed miserably. Throw in an abject inability to understand what makes the world tick in General Studies and I had passed one A Level out of 4. I should add that 27 years later in 1996 I passed French A Level after two years of most enjoyable and voluntary study at night school.

Had I been properly committed to my schoolbooks and not bothered with football, I could and should have passed ten O Levels, 4 A levels and gone to Oxford University and become, I dunno, a vicar. I would have been satisfied. It was nevertheless possible to be committed to sport and one's studies. All it required was a mature attitude and a deep resolution to achieve one's targets.

But I abandoned my studies in favour of sport. Football had been a false friend to me. But there were other sports and football was just a part of my misspent youth.

Chapter Seven – Horse Racing and Me

I have never been, nor ever will be, a betting man. Never had enough money to risk. But from the age of six the infant prodigy that I had become seemed to know everything there was to know about horse racing. My Mom and Dad used to have the Daily Mirror delivered to the door every morning except Sunday, when we had the News of the World and the People. I used to collect the papers from Bruton's newsagents which was almost opposite St Mary's Church, on a Sunday morning after church where I had been singing in the choir. There I would pay for our papers and those of my Dad's sister Auntie May, as she lived but fifty yards away from us; much to my Mom's consternation, as she could never work out why she couldn't pay for her own papers when she had a full time job, no mortgage and lived on her own. Neither could I if it came to it.

The Daily Mirror was a Socialist rag (which suited my parents) and as this impressionable six-year-old didn't do politics (still don't) I never got beyond the sports pages, so its political leanings were irrelevant. However, it provided excellent coverage of the football and cricket scores and embellished them with excellent pontifications from the sportswriters. And it was Newsboy who wrote the day's column on the horse racing page, doing it superbly.

The Mirror would print that day's race cards in full, accompanied by the choices of their two resident tipsters Newsboy and Bouverie. Being six years old I used to pronounce the latter in my instantly recognisable Bearwood accent 'Beau Veery' little realising it was pronounced 'Booviee' with a Maurice Chevalier-esque French accent. I used to think Newsboy was infallible, and Bouverie was some bloke from the pub because Newsboy's opinions were printed and Bouverie was not called upon for the written word.

The race card of the day's main meeting was always accompanied by a cartoon drawing of the head and cap of the jockey who was riding Newsboy's Best Bet, or Nap for the day.

I knew the names of the jockeys of that era off by heart. There were dozens of them. Lester Piggott was the indisputable king of jockeys; known as the Housewives' Choice because of the way all and sundry used to have their one and only bet of the year by lumping onto whatever Piggott was astride in the Epsom Derby.

His big rivals were the Aborigine Scobie Breasley, the brothers Doug and Eph Smith, more brothers in Joe and Manny Mercer, Harry Carr the Queen's jockey, and overseas jockeys like Roger Poincelet from France, or Ron Hutchinson and Bill Williamson from Australia. The jump jockey champion was the peerless Fred Winter who would receive token resistance from jockeys like Tim Molony and young upstarts like Michael Scudamore and Stan Mellor. Jump racing would take place on courses like Fontwell Park, Plumpton or Cartmel and I would have had more chance of finding the moon than locating these far-flung places on the map.

I would ride many a photo finish on the arm of the settee in the living room, bringing home my charge just on the line as Piggott's nag just failed to get up to defeat me on the finishing post. When I went to bed the same thing would happen as I rode many more finishes with my pillow scrunched up between my haunches. I even convinced one of my teachers at Bearwood Road that I used to ride in real horse races when I was away on the family summer holidays! I say convinced because she believed me (I was nine years old when I purveyed this blatant lie!).

There is a picture of me appearing to whip home a donkey on the beach at Llandudno in 1959 on the annual choirboys' outing, although the donkey was less than impressed, and could hardly be arsed to move in response to my urging.

In reality I couldn't ride a horse, although later on as teenagers me and my big mate Rob Gilding from Holly Lodge used to rent a couple of horses from a stable on the nearby Clent Hills when we were both well over the riding weight of professional jockeys.

From the age of six I also had a prodigious need to draw the objects of my interest, the horses and jockeys themselves. I would start by copying the action photos printed in the newspapers and then I realised I could reproduce these action shots from my own memory. For my age they were good as well, even though I say so myself, because I could the capture the shape and sometimes the musculature of the horses and the agility of the jockeys resplendent in their different coloured silks, although these were shades of lead pencil grey as black and white drawings and photos and not colour were the order of the day.

I would doodle like this for hours on end, and never tired of reproducing different versions of what were basically the same scenes. But this skill did not manifest itself in my becoming a talented artist at grammar school, as by the time I arrived there for Art lessons my disinterest in all things academic had rendered my drawing pretty damned ordinary.

I was terminally disillusioned when we were commissioned for Art homework to produce a still life drawing and I duly created a cartoon of my Dad's flat cap, complete with the intricate patterns of the material. I thought this was pretty good, still do in fact, but my Art Master rubbished it, probably because he didn't like me much and my interest in drawing waned, unfortunately, forever.

I had the racing calendar firmly fixed in my brain. The Flat season would start on the penultimate Monday in March with a three-day meeting at Lincoln, culminating in the first leg of the Spring Double, the Lincolnshire Handicap on the Wednesday, the final day of the meeting. The first race of the flat season was always a sprint race for apprentice jockeys only, so the winning apprentice could claim he was top of the jockey's table at least for half an hour until the next race when the professional riders got on board.

The second half of the week was taken up by a mixed meeting (Flat races and over the sticks) from the Aintree course in Liverpool, which staged the world famous Grand National on the Saturday (the second leg of the Spring Double), the most gruelling steeplechase in the world over 30 terrifying fences and run over 4 miles and 856 yards, to be precise.

These fences were monstrous birch fences, many of them with landing drops of over six feet and ditches which would claim many a horse and rider. I loved the Grand National, and would watch spellbound on the telly as anything up to fifty horses would set off into the Merseyside fog and on occasions only four would scramble home.

The rest had either fallen, unseated their riders, refused to jump, pulled up or run out of the course. Usually there would be at least one fatality amongst the horses due to the severity of the landings on many of the fences, but nobody seemed to mind, as it was all forgotten when the winning horse received its renowned police escort back to the unsaddling enclosure. I loved this race, and my excitement would build in the weeks preceding it with every little news item about one of the runners or the latest call-over of betting published by the Victoria Club. I didn't totally understand the full significance of what I was reading, but all this information was going in and staying in my overdeveloped brain.

Off course betting was illegal in this country until 1961, but what used to happen was that back street bookmakers abounded, staying one step ahead of the police, who would from time to time clamp down on any illegal bookie on their patch by issuing a few fines after a half-hearted raid on the bookie and his accomplices.

The system worked by having bookies' runners, people who would collect the bets from the punter and deliver them to the bookie. I believe my Dad used to take the occasional fine from the police for acting as a bookies' runner in order to throw them off the scent of the real bookie. He was, of course, well rewarded for his trouble, although in reality he didn't actually do any bookie's running.

The bookie in question used to run his operation from an office at the back of his house, which had a ticker tape machine bringing home the results of the races as they happened. I used to play at this house with the bookie's son, and was enthralled by the excitement and immediacy of the whole business. But in 1961 it all changed with the introduction of the Betting and Gaming Act, and everyone suddenly became legit.

But the Grand National was the race that enthralled and excited me. I could name all of the fences in order, especially the famous ones, such as Bechers Brook, 6th and 22nd fence, Valentine's Brook, 9th and 25th, The Chair, 15th, and the Water Jump, 16th. BBC Grandstand gave the race hours of live build-up, and I recall seeing the famous 1956 National where the Queen Mother's horse Devon Loch jumped an imaginary fence yards from the line and promptly sat down, allowing the horse ESB with the disbelieving Dave Dick on board to scamper past for an improbable victory. Devon Loch's jockey Dick Francis was so broken by this occurrence that he virtually retired on the spot and 'wasted' the rest of his life by writing dozens of bestselling thrillers and living in Jamaica!

1957 saw the veteran champion jump jockey Fred Winter pilot Sundew home, Mr What led home only three other finishers in the fog in 1958 giving Arthur Freeman a winning ride, and 1959 saw Oxo and Michael Scudamore triumph. And so on. Every renewal of the National stayed with me for almost the whole year, until it came around again and I relived each race many times over.

I remember on Easter Monday 1957 at my cousin Jean's wedding, when I, being a mere six years old, didn't have a fat lot of interest in the nuptials, so I sat at the wedding reception with the Daily Mirror open, oblivious to what was going on around me. Bearing in mind my tender years I could read like an adult, so I was devouring what was going to be happening that afternoon at the races.

The main Easter meeting was a Flat meeting at Kempton Park and I recall advising my Uncle Bill, who had enquired good-naturedly where I would recommend him to place his hard-earned cash, to lump it all on a horse named Hornbeam, ridden, I believe by Joe Mercer, in the day's big race. He nearly fell off his chair because this advice had come from such a small human being; even though proudly, I was a blood relative and I think it won and was one of the better horses of the day.

History could easily be checked to see if I was right, but I remember several of the big names at the time. There were horses like Loppylugs, which won the Cesarewitch Stakes or the Cambridgeshire Handicap at Newmarket in the autumn. There was a horse called Hilarion Tempest after which I named a footballing marble; a veteran chaser called Crudwell, which won loads of races over the sticks. I remember the inaugural running of the Hennessey Gold Cup at Newbury in 1957, where Mandarin (with Gerry Madden up) made up a phenomenal deficit to overhaul Taxidermist on the line in front of an amazed telly audience on BBC Grandstand.

The Epsom Derby occupied as similar a place in my mind as did the National. This was a mile and a half race for three-year-old colts on the switchback track at Epsom Downs, and was watched the world over.

As with the National, every snippet of news or the latest call over of the odds had me devouring all the information from the Daily Mirror as the big day approached. The winner of the Derby was feted as the Champion horse of the year, and the Daily Mirror next day would show a front-on picture of the horses as they finished the race up the notorious hill to the winning post. The Derby had thrown up some spectacular news stories, none more so than when the suffragette Emily Davison threw herself in front of the King's horse in the 1910 race and was killed by the flying hooves.

In later times the champion jockey Sir Gordon Richards had striven for about thirty years to ride a winner of the Derby despite winning some four thousand-odd other races, and he at last obliged in 1953 on Pinza. This was the year of the Queen's Coronation and the jockey was knighted for his achievement. Coincidentally, the month before had seen Sir Stanley Matthews, England's first legendary footballer, at last win an FA Cup winner's medal with Blackpool.

The first Derby I can remember was in 1957 when Lester Piggott steered Crepello home, then two days later won on Carrozza in The Oaks, the fillies Derby, to complete the double. Crepello was one of nine winning rides Piggott piloted home in the Derby. Hard Ridden duly obliged in 1958 under Charlie Smirke, a veteran Irish jockey and the Derby had me spellbound, as the years memorably rolled by. My favourite Piggott Derby winner was Nijinsky, in 1970 and I can still picture his phenomenal sprint to the line, leaving all and sundry in his wake; and I swear the horse's hooves never touched the ground!

I was hooked on the statistics of the sport and used to chronicle my own records of the season's flat race jockey victories as the Daily Mirror would only catalogue the top ten riders every Monday. I waited each year in vain for a jockey to top the magical 200 winner mark; but it didn't happen, Lester Piggott seemed to be the perennial champ, interspersed with occasional titles won by Doug Smith or Scobie Breasley.

One Christmas when I was a small boy Santa Claus paid homage to my study of this Sport of Kings when he bought me 'Escalado', the replica horse racing game. (Can I just throw in here that a horse called Santa Claus won the Derby in the mid-sixties. Uncanny eh?) Escalado was broadly similar to those penny betting machines one finds at funfairs, where one bets on a jockey's colours and the horses make their way mechanically, and very unsteadily, to the winning post. Whereupon if one has backed the winning nag, then the machine coughs up your winnings. Not addictive but great fun.

'Escalado' had a piece of green canvas, stretched by elastic bands at either end, and a wooden handle which one turned at speed causing vibrations, making the metal horses move along the track towards the winning post, navigating 'hurdles' along the way. These were were rows of studs in the canvas track with gaps for the horses' hooves to bump their way through. Enormous fun, particularly on a Christmas night when the family are around and Uncle Bill has had a couple and he can pretend he is down at the bookies'.

Major drawback of 'Escalado' was that if you were the poor sod deputed to turn the wooden handle then it wore a blistered hole in your thumb very quickly which machettied its way painfully down to the bone. But I believe 'Escalado' is still available in some shops in some form, and can definitely be bought on the internet.

Events of that time when I was a small boy come flooding back, such as when A J (Alec) Russell won eleven races out of twelve during the two-day meeting at the now defunct Bogside track in Ayrshire. That was a feat I still find hard to comprehend.

I remember the high drama and tragedy when Manny Mercer was killed during a race at Royal Ascot in 1959. He was at the top of his game and I could not take this news in for some time as I didn't fully understand what death meant. Tracks came and went and racecourses like the aforementioned Bogside, Bromford Bridge in Birmingham, Castle Irwell in Manchester, Rothbury in Northumberland, Woore (in Kent?), Hurst Park and Alexandra Park (both in London), Stockton, and Lincoln all staged their final meetings.

Whilst I was on holiday with my parents at Torquay in 1964, we went to a jump race meeting at Newton Abbot, and Dad and I walked to the start for one of the races. Whilst we were there, we heard the jockeys, who were walking their mounts around, discussing how the race was going to pan out, who would take up the running, and virtually who would contest the finish.

I am not saying they were cheating (that word again) but it destroyed something inside me, and the child who knew too much about horse racing gradually lost interest in the sport. And I am glad because if horse racing had taken hold of me in the same way that football and cricket did, then I dread to think what would have happened.

Some years later, when I was on cricket tour with work colleagues from Barclays Bank, where I worked after leaving school, a couple of the lads, who were obviously quite heavy backers of horses, would converse with each other in the same language as that used by Newsboy in the Daily Mirror and it made me feel quite uneasy.

It all seemed too risky to let horse racing get a hold of you like that. And these lads worked with money all day and every day.

Yes, horse racing and I would have been unwelcome bedfellows, and I let my knowledge of the Turf dissipate before I was too much older. I now have barely a passing interest in the sport and have even become mildly disinterested in the Grand National and the Epsom Derby, but I content myself with the Cheltenham Gold Cup, which is my favourite race. The roar when the leading horse lands safely over the final fence I believe is unparalleled in sport. My misspent youth included horse racing, but I saved myself from it before I let it get a grip of me.

Chapter Eight – Cycling and Me

At this point I am going to talk about the sport of cycling, which, in the context of this book, is completely incongruous, because I actually took up competitive cycling at the age of 57, during my Misspent Dotage. Time trialling immediately had me gripped, and there, delightfully, I remain to this day. It is known as the race of truth because it is you and your body against the clock, and although each race takes one to your individual pain threshold, I love it and it completely and utterly makes me tick. But really and truly it all began in the year of 1959, when I was eight years old and older brother Roger was fourteen.

He and three of his mates from Holly Lodge started riding, and they equipped and fettled some really good racing bikes on which they rode together. Roger would ride to school and back daily, a five-mile round trip as well, as doing a twice-daily paper round, which involved carting on his bike the incredibly heavy delivery bag. I know this for a fact because I followed exactly in his footsteps, when I reached the age of fourteen, as I tried to follow him in so many other different activities.

This intense riding rendered him incredibly fit, and it was not long before he and his mates had joined the nearby Halesowen Cycling Club, with its 400-metre outdoor banked velodrome. The club remains to this day the only cycling club in Britain which owns its own track, as local councils usually own the others and rent them to the clubs. Being in the fortunate position of being the only cycling club in the immediate locality with such a facility, then it became an elite club, and an oasis for the best riders in the area.

Roger started training with the club members and improved rapidly, by training with and against some of the best riders in the country. At this time the local superstar was a rider named Roy Hurdley, who hailed from West Bromwich.

Hurdley was an elite sprinter, competing at the highest amateur level, being selected, I believe, in the England team for the Commonwealth Games in Kingston, Jamaica in 1962. Training with the best meant that Roger was getting to their level, and when he was competing either at Halesowen, or other local tracks in the area, my ever-supporting parents (and me) would be there to cheer him on. I was only a young whippersnapper but Roger seemed to me to be quite good at this cycling lark and was winning races.

He would of course be competing at junior, or schoolboy level, and we all watched spellbound as the top senior riders duked it out on the track in the sprints, which were a cross between chess and wrestling on two wheels – and certainly not an activity for the faint-hearted!

Top riders like Karl Barton, from my dad's workplace, Coventry, Lloyd Binch and our local hero Roy Hurdley were all on view, and Roger was rubbing shoulders with them. He would buy Cycling Weekly, which I would devour with as much enthusiasm as he did, and the names of these riders which appeared in print were firmly etched in my brain, so to see them in the flesh was a great thrill. I knew all the different types of races like the individual pursuit, the devil-take-the hindmost and the sprints.

The National Schoolboy Championship which was a sprint competition for Under-15 schoolboys was Roger's target. He figured he was in with a fighting chance, as he was outsprinting all his local rivals and he was incredibly fit and focussed. This now becomes the story Roger still dines out on.

As luck would have it when the Championship date came around, Roger missed it because he was ill, and the blue riband of National Schoolboy Champion was placed around the neck of a lad named Pete Jenner from Portsmouth. Jenner showed up at the now long-disappeared Salford Bridge track in Birmingham. The rules of the sprint were that riders raced for three laps of the track, in groups of either two, three or up to six competitors, with the first two laps being completed at snail's pace as, to mix metaphors, they played cat and mouse with each other, waiting for someone to twitch a muscle and make the break for home. The less time one spent sprinting, then the more energy one had for these lung-busting finishes. Times were measured only over the last 200 high-speed metres. I was positioned with Mom and Dad above the banking of the final bend looking directly down the final straight.

Roger and Pete Jenner set off in a bunch of six, which number was always a recipe for impending disaster. They cat and moused their way around the first lap; and the second lap began with the six of them bunched up and starting to crank up the speed, as the nerves started jangling, on and off the bikes. As they hit the final bend for the penultimate time right in front of me, one rider made his bid for home and went for the long sprint. The other five reacted to this move in a split second, but there was an awful coming together of metal and flesh as four of the bikes smashed into each other at high speed.

There was blood, gore and shredded metal everywhere, and I watched on in horror as one bike frame actually snapped in two. But Roger and one other rider had escaped the carnage, and set off to sprint the remaining lap and a half to the finishing line. They went hell for leather around the track, picking their way through the debris only thirty seconds or so after it had happened, as they came around that final bend one last time; and Roger emerged victorious by taking the chequered flag. Pete Jenner was nowhere. Roger tells me he beat him again in their only other meeting, so his after dinner boast is that but for illness, he and not Pete Jenner should have been National Schoolboy Champion.

From my point of view, I used to accompany Roger and Dad to the training sessions at Halesowen velodrome, and was persuaded onto my brother's bike one day to try it out.

I think I was ten years old. A track bike has a fixed wheel and no brakes, so if you don't know what you are doing you could maim yourself.

I didn't know what I was doing. However, serious injury was avoided as the legendary Roy Hurdley held me up on the bike, and kept me upright, as I turned the pedals. I didn't like it much. Ironically, fifty years later I was to do thousands of laps of this same Halesowen track, in preparation for the World Masters Track Championships at Manchester, in which I rode on three occasions, securing eighth place one year in the 2000 metres Individual pursuit.

Indeed, for three minutes I was the virtual world champion, after I rode against a Scotsman named Jim Robertson in the first heat and I beat him, setting the fastest time (obviously). Needless to say, everyone else taking part beat my time. I have photographic evidence of the electronic scoreboard at that moment showing me as number one in the world. Who said the camera doesn't lie?

As the time was approaching when I would be going to Holly Lodge Grammar School, which was a good bike ride away, Roger was given some money by Mom and Dad and was tasked with building me my first bike, which he did with great skill. I believe they reasoned they would recoup the cost of the bike in saved bus fares; and their logic was sound. All parts were brand new on this bike. which was built around a maroon coloured Viking frame, and when it was completed, I loved it. The bike was a huge credit to my brother, who had inherited Dad's mechanical skills, and which had completely by-passed me. Roger always said that I could ride a bike but hadn't a b****y clue how it worked.

I used to ride this bike a lot, and one evening during the summer I turned left into Rutland Road off the Bearwood Road and, with a habit I still dangerously have to this day, with my head down I rode straight into the rear bumper of a parked car, which I believe was a VW Beetle. I was tossed over the handlebars headfirst, and landed on my cheek on the boot of said car. Miraculously that was the only injury I suffered, albeit only a slight one, and with my bike appearing to be still in one piece, I carefully set off to ride the short distance home.

With my untrained eye the bike looked fine, but my brother spotted a v-shaped kink in the frame where the crossbar meets the front fork, and pronounced the bike an item of scrap. Roger was disgusted with me of course, but Mom and Dad gave him some more money, and he built a second bike from new for me. It was this second bike which did yeoman service, transporting me to school and back and on my paper rounds.

But football and cricket were to keep cycling off my list of priorities. I gave up my paper round, this being principally because I was keeping the money that Walsall Football Club were giving me, as well as my poor brother also giving me pocket money from his taxed income. (Believe me, I am eternally grateful, if I had been the older sibling, I would have done the same for him.) My cycling career to all intents and purposes, came to an end.

There it remained until the first day of September 2007, when I, at the age of 56, climbed back on a bike, and, at the time of writing, there I have remained. Believe it or not, if I were to shuffle off this mortal coil tomorrow (whatever that means) then cycling would be the sport that has given me the most pleasure, and the biggest thrills. But my cycling career is a story for another day, and another tome, so I will leave it there.

Chapter Nine – Other Sports and Me

It would be appropriate at this point to reflect on the other sports which this juvenile sporting obsessive dabbled in without succumbing to their temptations, before I move on to the game of cricket and its effect on my whole being.

Let us consider tennis, or Lawn Tennis in particular. The Lawn Tennis season in the UK lasts for about six weeks in high midsummer, due principally to the vagaries of our lousy climate. But because most great sporting events had their origins in these sceptred isles, then we are privileged to stage the world's greatest tennis tournament, at the All England Lawn Tennis and Croquet Club in Wimbledon, South West London.

This tournament has always been the province of BBC Television, who from the beginning of time have provided dawn to dusk wall to wall coverage of the matches; and the whole viewing populace of the country is glued to its TV screens for its entire fortnight's duration. This has a curious effect on the hitherto rational UK inhabitant. During Wimbledon fortnight, every home in the land seems mysteriously to produce tennis rackets of varying ages from absolutely nowhere, and the parks, and previously totally underused tennis courts, are crammed with people who have suddenly become tennis afficionados on the grandest of scales.

Me and my band of mates were, as you will have surmised, no exception to these goings on, and Lightwoods Park would be the scene of our own Wimbledon tournaments on the same scope and vision of our Test Matches and football games. In Lightwoods Park we were blessed with two enclosed hard tennis courts, and in the Extension we actually had about five grass courts side by side.

These were available all the year round, totally unused all the year round, and usually unplayable all the year round through weather conditions; but of course, in Wimbledon fortnight they suddenly became probably the second busiest suite of lawn tennis courts in the land. There was even a tennis pavilion for the use of the grass court players but we never actually saw it open.

We also had access to three flat tennis court sized grassed areas in the Park opposite the top of my road, which were separated by small bankings and we called these the Bumps. Games would take place on the Bumps without, of course, nets, so we put down jumpers to mark where the net would be and played on regardless.

This removed the tedious activity of trying to start a rally by actually serving the ball successfully over the net; and many a game, when we had illegally actually taken over one of the Park's proper courts; could be lost by the serving of four successive double faults. When we did use the real courts, we would play there until evicted, or more accurately chased off by the parkkeepers, who didn't like the next generation of sporting superstars learning their trade on their parklands.

I think they would have been happier if the only users of the Park had been the local worm population. One of the parkies looked like Hitler, and he had a pronounced limp from an old war wound, which we assume he acquired whilst fighting for our side even though he looked like Public Enemy Number One. Anyway, his limp meant we could always outrun him, once he had made the tactical error of shouting at us to 'bugger off' before he had physically arrived at the court gates.

So the nation would be gripped during the tournament fortnight by Wimbledon fever, only to relapse into the tennis equivalent of a coma the moment that the final tennis ball had been struck on Centre Court; and me and my mates were no exception. It is no wonder that we produce so few world class players in this country when 99.999% of the inhabitants are totally incapable of serving the bloody ball over the net.

The net merely seemed an obstacle put there to prevent a decent game of tennis developing, similar to attempting to play football with a 40-foot high brick wall adorning the halfway line, put there to prevent a decent game of football breaking out. I don't mean these comments in a derogatory way, but how often do you see an aesthetically pleasing game of tennis when strolling through the park? It is a difficult game to play well.

Tennis for us lads was unfortunately only always a short-lived aberration on an annual basis. Areas like Bearwood and Smethwick are extremely unlikely ever to produce the next Andy Murray or Jo Konta, due to top class tennis facilities and organisation and availability of elite coaching being low on the borough's priorities. (Ann Jones, the Wimbledon Ladies' Champion of the 60s can be seen walking her dog in Warley Woods to this day, but she lives in nearby Edgbaston, which is affluent enough to stage a world level Ladies Professional tournament annually at the Priory Club). Wimbledon and Lawn Tennis are a bit like having a heavy cold for a fortnight, and then recovering without falling prey to such an annoying virus for another twelve months.

I should at this point state that I have actually been to the Wimbledon Championships twice in the last two years for the first time in my (sporting) life and it was surprisingly, a hugely enjoyable experience. When I was there the first time my big mate Trev Boyle, who lives in Paris, rang me on my mobile phone and enquired "Hello Brian, where are you?" When I replied that I was at the tennis at Wimbledon he said, somewhat startled, "What the bloody hell are you doing there?" He still knows me after all these years! I rest my case on Tennis.

Golf was a strange one. I lived less than a mile away from a beautifully appointed nine hole municipal golf course in Warley Woods, but I didn't set foot in the place until I was in my early twenties and working at Barclays Bank, when I let the game get a hold on me by playing nine holes every Saturday morning with my Assistant Manager from the Bank.

He, Dave Claridge, was a lovely guy, some thirty years my senior, but he was nevertheless a good friend to me, and even came to watch me play some Saturday afternoons for the Bank football team when I was banging in a few goals for them. In truth I loved playing those nine holes, but being outside the golf course at six o'clock in the morning on a Saturday to queue up for tee-off time meant that frequently I was hot footing it to a Birmingham League cricket match, with scarcely a pause for breath. Shades of my Holly Lodge to Walsall or Shrewsbury Town timetables, and I am afraid golf had to go after a few enjoyable years as nothing was going to interfere with my dedication to cricket.

Mom and Dad had an unfortunate experience on a golf course on one occasion when I was about ten or eleven years old, as one day we stopped for a picnic lunch in the middle of Ludlow racecourse which, on non-race days, plied its trade as Ludlow Golf Club. We were tucking into yet more of Mom's lovingly-prepared sarnies when a cry of 'Fore' went up from the middle distance. As neither Mom, Dad or I knew what this hearty rendering represented, Mom was suddenly struck a quite nasty and painful blow on the elbow by the fast travelling golf ball. This led to us beating a hasty retreat from the golf course so as to avoid any of us being mortally wounded by these golf ball missiles.

I used to watch the golf on BBC Grandstand only because it was another sport played with a round ball, but trying to get a tiny golf ball into a hole some four hundred or so yards away with a metal stick in four shots seemed beyond the remit of a little Herbert like me. So I contented myself with cramming all the latest golf news into my head, as opposed to any pretensions to actually learning to play the game.

So that was golf; but table tennis was an interesting sport. I used to play the game from the age of eight at Choirboys' Club on Tuesday nights after choir practice, and us choristers were all quite adept at the sport. When I got to Holly Lodge, I entered the ping-pong tournament for my year group, thinking (as usual) that I would probably smash my way to the title by virtue of my comparative longevity in the sport at the club: but how wrong (as usual) can you be?

I was drawn in the first round against a lad named Chris Bedford or "Crippin" as he was known, when later we became colleagues in the school football team. Crippin's Dad was a renowned competitive pigeon fancier, and he once resorted to breaking up his own wooden chairs to throw at an idle champion pigeon who was sitting on their roof at home, taking absolutely no notice whatsoever, instead of coming down to get his finish recorded and thus enabling a big cash prize to be won.

Crippin wiped the floor with me, then added insult to injury, or in his case illness, by collapsing with appendicitis before he could play his second-round match. He couldn't have had the forethought to have collapsed a half hour or so earlier to give me a bye to the next round, now could he?

Our German teacher was an England Junior table tennis international named Derek Backhouse, who could play anyone at ping-pong in the school with a frying pan, as well as serving the ball to you and telling you which wall you were going to hit as you attempted to return his serve. This was by virtue of the disgusting amounts of spin he imparted to his serves. He was a star with the pimpled bat in his hands to us awestruck schoolboys,

I tried to get back into Mr Backhouse's German lessons by taking on extra tuition, having dropped the subject for Biology; yet another nonsensical decision of mine. My earlier attempts at German had led to my translation of a German passage in an exam which contained the illogical phrase "He opened the door and horses and bicycles flew past". That conjured up a picture, but was hopelessly inaccurate. So much so, that Mr Backhouse would frequently read out this translation of mine at the end of lessons if we had a moment to spare, much to his, and particularly Trev Boyle's amusement. To this day I end my emails to Trev with words 'Horses and bicycles' or simply 'H and B'.

If we had a minute to spare at the end of Tadpole Mason's French lessons, he would get me to do a couple of my impersonations of other members of staff, including himself.

You can see my talents were all directed in the wrong direction. Tadpole used to get Trev Boyle and myself to take his bets to the local betting shop, and we would visit the transport café next door for a coffee before returning to school. One day I was standing at the counter flicking a tanner (sixpenny piece) repeatedly in the air, and it didn't land back in my hand but in a navvie's mug of Bovril standing next to me. Trev and I didn't hang around long enough to gauge his reaction. I hope the recovered tanner would have covered the cost of a replacement drink!

I briefly turned out for the table tennis team put into a local league by my brother's Youth Club which he supervised after he had qualified as a Youth Leader, but I don't recall uprooting any trees in that sphere either so regrettably, if not predictably, table tennis became another sport tested, but rejected, through lack of any tangible expertise on my part.

Likewise snooker, the other sport at which we used to play religiously, excuse the pun, at Choirboys Club. We played on a half-sized snooker table on which the balls had difficulty in running a true course, but we loved our weekly go with the cues on the green baize. If you had a break of three balls, then you were feted by your peers as being a worthy successor to the legendary world snooker champion of the time Joe Davis, who was to snooker what Stirling Moss was to motor racing.

Snooker became a useful pastime in later years, particularly on the numerous cricket tours I went on as a player, but again I never developed any great skill at a game I did love watching on the TV. That was curious in itself, in that snooker, a game which centres on potting the differently coloured balls in a predetermined order, was watched by a spellbound audience on black and white telly, as again colour broadcasts were some years away. This led to the legendary commentator Ted Lowe coming up with the classic line "For those of you watching in black and white the red is behind the green". You couldn't script it could you?

It was only when the medium of colour became widely available in the early 1970s that the BBC had the brainwave of sponsoring a TV- based one-frame competition called Pot Black that the popularity of this sport rocketed. The very first winner of the Pot Black competition was a Smethwick professional snooker player named Graham Miles and he brought into the bank on Cape Hill, Smethwick, where I was working, his winner's cheque about a month before the final frame was due to be broadcast, so he had to swear me to secrecy. Miles was a good enough pro to be the defeated finalist in the World Snooker Championship at around that time.

But again, snooker was another sport which came nowhere near interfering with my misspent youth, as the damage was being safely done by other sports!

Hockey flickered ever so briefly on my sporting landscape. At Holly Lodge the Girls School First XI at Hockey would have an annual challenge match against the Boys School First XI football team. The activity chosen was, of course, hockey which any right-thinking person would think would even things up somewhat, but no! This particular contest was never going to be an even battle of the sexes. Because battle became the operative word. The girls saw this as their opportunity, probably a once in a lifetime opportunity, to knock seven shades of you know what out of the boys. And to make matters worse, although we were all armed with a hockey stick, we, the boys, didn't have the first idea how to use them, whereas the girls turned into a screaming horde of St Trinian's on the first whistle, wielding their sticks as weapons.

As captain of the Boys team I tossed the coin to decide ends before the game. Having duly won the toss, I selected which goal we would attack, only to be met by my opposite number who snarled something from behind lipsticked lips to the effect that they were going to attack us, regardless of which way we were kicking, sorry, sticking, or whatever the correct expression was. The game commenced, and was a constant niggle fest from the very start and as us boys didn't know what the rules were, this fact alone giving the girls an unfair advantage.

Ankles were being tapped and fingers smacked by females wielding their hockey sticks like shillelaghs until my moment came.

I think it was my mate Malcolm Bailey, also known as Bill, who crossed the ball to me from the right wing, and it bounced up invitingly for me in my predatory position at centre forward. I glanced goalward briefly, and saw the girls' goalkeeper, a buxom wench clad in goalkeeping pads and with her masses of unkempt hair tied (unsuccessfully) to keep it off her snarling visage. As the ball reached me, I met it on the volley as if I was hitting a cricket ball with some velocity to the boundary, and it screamed past the startled goalie into one of the few vacant areas she could not guard and smashed into the roof of the net.

Whereupon I turned to face my relieved teammates as this was the opening goal and we were on our way to sticking it to the girls when the lady referee, (or was she an umpire?) came skipping daintily over towards me and disallowed the goal because I had used the wrong side of my stick. "What" I enquired disbelievingly. She told me in no uncertain terms that one could only hit the ball with one side of the stick and I had infringed that particular rule and the goal would not stand. "You might have told me that before the game started!" I said to her and she said "Well, you never asked, did you?" and with that requested the goalie, who by now had picked her not inconsiderable frame off the floor, to restart the game.

I think the game ended in a goalless draw but the game of hockey did absolutely nothing to endear itself to me that particular afternoon so it was binned along with a few other sports I was trying.

I think I said Rugby would not be mentioned again, but I am going to give it a little more coverage. Holly Lodge Grammar School was first and foremost a football playing school. The large influx of Welsh teachers into Smethwick schools in those post-war years meant that there was an ever-growing band of men who had sung 'Bread of Heaven' with gusto at Welsh home Rugby Union internationals staged at Cardiff Arms Park.

They were prevented by a higher authority from introducing the code of Rugby at every school in the borough until one lunch time at the Lodge a game of Union was organised by one member of the teaching staff, who was obviously a son of Owen Glendower, although I never found out for what team or in what position Glendower played.

I was asked to participate in this 'ere game and refused point blank. I kept on refusing until I was persuaded by my Bearwood Road and Holly Lodge older colleague Kevin Jordan to play, as he had fallen irretrievably under the spell of this game. So I turned out, and was totally mystified by the ovoid shape of the ball, which meant that even if one had the ball playing skills of Lionel Messi and Cristiano Ronaldo combined and multiplied by ten, if the ball bounced its own way, which it frequently did as it seemed to have a mind of its own, you were completely and utterly stuffed. Add in the factor that there were some seriously unsavoury characters opposing you who wanted to separate you and your vital organs from the ball as painfully as possible, then I was as close to signing up to be a Trappist monk as you could get when kick-off approached.

I thought with my footballing speed I could catch the ovum (not totally certain if that is the right word?) and with a jink and a sidestep could outsprint everyone on my way to scoring a try. Wrong in every way. Someone threw the ball to me, and I duly caught it and set off on the predetermined jinkfest.

After completing less than one stride, my mate Kev grabbed me round the waist and proceeded to dump me unceremoniously shoulder first on the rock-hard ground, thus spilling the ball, and very nearly my guts, in one smooth motion. Even I know that this was a spear tackle, and would have earned him an instant red card and probably a lengthy suspension under the current interpretation of the rules of the game. But Kev had always been a man on a mission, and his mission was to give me a baptism in this hellish game, which would stand me in good stead for the rest of my undoubted longevity as a Rugby Union practitioner.

I lay motionless on the floor and my brain suddenly had all the oxygen drained from it as I considered lapsing into a comatose state. The game was eventually stopped, as my lifeless body was proving an obstacle to the players who saw me as part of the field of play and I was helped slowly to the sidelines, nursing a severely bruised shoulder and muttering to myself that I would never darken a Rugby pitch again as long as I lived; which felt as though it was going to be about twenty minutes. I have kept that promise to myself, quite easily.

My big mate Rob Gilding, one of the stars of that famed Smethwick Under 15 football team and rabble-rouser par excellence for Tupelo FC, turned to the game of Union in his mid-twenties with some success, much to my admiration of him. At the time of writing his oldest son Jack has been a professional Rugby Union player for over ten years, playing for clubs in England, Wales, Scotland and Italy. Kev took up the game on a permanent basis the moment he dumped me on my shoulder and was instrumental in setting up the Warley Rugby Club, which he served with distinction until he passed away some five years ago.

Right, I have finally got the game of Rugby Union (of which I have never understood the rules anyway) off my shoulder, sorry, chest. Moving on.

Athletics was, of course, synonymous with the Olympic Games, and true to form, during the 1960 Olympiad staged in Rome we held our own version which ran concurrently. I lived in an end-terrace house which was on a square of a block comprising four roads (Milcote Road, St Marys Road, Wigorn Road and Loxley Road). This gave us a perfect track on which to stage our kids' version of the Olympic Games.

As per usual I took on the role of the Baron Pierre de Coubertin, who I think was the French bloke instrumental in founding the modern Olympiad in Athens in 1896, from where the quadrennial sporting bonanza has mushroomed to its present uncontrollable state.

Our block was the natural amphitheatre for the track events, and I remember my mate Rod gloriously winning the 10,000 metres by doing 40 laps anti-clockwise (the correct direction) of the square to joyfully claim his gold medal, which we made from milk bottle tops and pieces of ribbon filched from my Mom's sewing basket. In truth each side of the square was probably 75 metres giving a lap of 300, as opposed to 400 metres like a proper running track. But we didn't know this as we watched Rod Lucas pound his way to his sweaty, 40 lapped glory run.

One of the shining stars of the Rome Olympiad was the black American female sprinter Wilma Rudolph, who blazed her way to a brilliant double sprint gold in the 100 and 200 metre dashes. Our sprint races were held opposite my house on the straight uninterrupted stretch of Milcote Road pavement, and I think my mate Mickey Carroll emulated Ms Rudolph with a similar sprint double to earn more bottle topped medallions.

But like Wimbledon, the Olympics occupied our sporting minds only for the two weeks with which they occupied everyone else's and normal service was soon to be resumed in Lightwoods Park, much to the relief of our long-suffering neighbours who complained about the noise, having not been forewarned about the coming of the Bearwood Olympics. Which was a good job, as I wasn't much cop at this Athletics lark at the tender age of nine, even though at the age of 33 I was to complete the Wolverhampton Marathon in a time of 3 hours 33 minutes 45 seconds, a feat which I believe classed me as a runner and not a jogger.

Again, Athletics was a sport which I watched on telly, hoovering up the information on offer, but never feeling the need, or the inclination to participate.

Swimming was a slightly different kettle of fish, to use a contrived but nevertheless watery metaphor. I learnt to swim on the family holiday in Llandudno in the blazing summer of 1959.

There were a couple of paddling pools in the middle of the promenade which were filled with salty sea water but which didn't have those dratted waves that used to make trying to swim in the sea nigh-on impossible. I believe these pools are still there and in full use.

Dad's car, which I think was an Austin Seven (I must put my cards on the table at this juncture to state that I haven't got a clue what I am on about when it comes to cars – my father's mechanical genes having sidestepped me to save themselves for future generations of Joneses). The seats did not comprise padded upholstery, as they do these days, but were actually given their shape and comfort by giant inflatable inner tubes. Dad removed the tube from his seat, gave it a careful reinflation, and then wrapped it round me with the instruction to get in the paddling pool and, well, paddle.

I laboured up and down finding this rubber contraption which was engulfing me more of a hindrance than a help, but eventually the miracle happened, and when Dad unravelled me from its clutches and repeated the instruction to paddle, I did just that, staying afloat. There is a picture of me in my swimming trunks relaxing in said paddling pool with the tentacles of the giant rubber inner tube floating on the surface between my knees, as if I have just suffered a painful and sudden external hernia.

So, I was off and running as a swimmer (mixed metaphor alert). Bearwood Road School took us for weekly swimming lessons at the palatial Thimblemill Baths, a walk of but 250 yards from our school gates, and my prowess as a swimmer duly increased as I obtained certificates for Third Class, for swimming one width of this one hundred foot bath, Second Class, for swimming one whole length, and finally First Class, for swimming further than one length and diving into the pool without headbutting the bottom and returning to the surface still alive. Achieving First Class meant that you were rewarded with a free pass to the baths, which meant that this was a frequent place to go for me and my mates, especially during the spells of inclement weather.

During the winter Thimblemill Baths closed to swimming, and was converted into a dance hall by boarding over the drained pool. And it was here in the winter of 1961/62 that the Beatles performed a concert when they were still the Silver Beatles (John Paul George and Pete Best – this was pre Ringo) which was only a matter of months before they hit the UK charts for the first time in September 1962 (the same month that I first entered Holly Lodge Grammar School) with 'Love Me Do' which was the springboard – yet another tedious swimming connected pun – to their everlasting worldwide fame and fortune.

Interestingly, BBC Grandstand televised a Great Britain Swimming international live from Thimblemill Baths around that period. I attended as a paying spectator, seeing for the first time how TV cameras brought these sporting events into our own homes via that tiny flickering TV screen (or at least our Cossor set was, both tiny and flickering).

I was not a competitive swimmer by any means, and I could only swim breaststroke, as I found front and back crawl beyond me by virtue of being totally incapable of coordinating my limbs to help propel me in a forward direction. Curiously, I could swim butterfly, that most knackering of swimming strokes, but would have had difficulty in completing a full length, having swallowed most of the pool in my endeavours to get from one end to the other and being unable to close my mouth whilst doing so.

This 'ability' at breaststroke meant that I was pressganged every year by my house master to represent Warwick House in the annual School Swimming Sports breaststroke race. This was a one-length affair and the contestants were me - not a member of the school swimming team, and seven other amphibious creatures - all members of the school swimming team. My whole raison d'etre for competing in this race was to earn a single solitary point for my house, which I did by finishing last. Every year. The whole school of course witnessed this annual sacrifice on my part, but I didn't totally disgrace myself, as one year I finished my lap before the swimming pool attendants had turned the lights off and gone home.

So swimming, like the other sports in this chapter failed dismally to make any sort of contribution to my misspent youth.

Chapter Ten – Cricket at the Primary School

I have left the sport of cricket last in this novella (pretentious), because its influence over me extended right up to my 60th birthday at the end of the 2010 season, when, without knowing it at the time, I played what is to date my last competitive game. I say without knowing it because I didn't tell Harborne Cricket Club, for whom I was playing, when I would next be available, and that was because cycling, or more precisely time trialling, took me over completely. The game in question, which became the last of a cricketing career that spanned fifty-two seasons (1959-2010 inclusive) was for Harborne against Bewdley Cricket Club; and joyously, my two nephews Simon and Ben (my brother Roger's lads) were in the Bewdley team. Both, I can proudly report were super batters and have kept up the Jones family tradition of making big scores when at the crease.

The last ball I ever received was from Bewdley's slow left arm spinner, and he turned one on me, as they say these days it grew big on me, and I ladled it tamely to short mid-wicket, who routinely completed a not too difficult catch. I do remember earlier in this final innings I played a sumptuous square cut, which raced off my bat backward of square on the offside for my last ever boundary. That, as it transpired, was a fitting way to depart the stage.

When I was growing up in the mid-1950s many sports were still evolving, and there were some momentous occasions which stand proudly against anything ever achieved. Two spring to mind. In 1954 Roger Bannister became the first athlete to break the four-minute mile at the University of Oxford Iffley Road track. I believe this achievement was voted the most iconic sporting event in the whole of the twentieth century, and its magnitude loomed large over all of the sporting world for the next few years, if not longer.

The other astonishing feat of this era was that of Jim Laker taking nineteen Australian wickets for 90 runs in the Old Trafford Test Match in 1956. I was three when Bannister ran himself into the ground as well as the history books, and five when Laker spun Australia to their doom. But my early memories of these wonderful moments were, well, foggy to say the least.

From a very early age I used to pretend in our back garden that I was a great cricketer. Although I don't know to whom I was demonstrating this talent, yet I knew there was someone called Bannister who was very good at something or other. Problem was, I was thinking of Ken Barrington, the Surrey and England batsman, whose name was being mentioned more and more on the radio and in the press as his career was burgeoning.

In the mid-50s Surrey were in the middle of a run of seven successive County Championship titles, and Ken Bannister, sorry, Ken Barrington, was one of their top performers. Likewise, the bowler Jim Laker had secreted himself into my subconscious to such an extent that I had heard that our neighbouring school, and immense rivals, Abbey Road Primary, had a demon bowler called Laker – Trevor Laker. Deep down I was thinking hasn't this kid recently taken nineteen wickets in a Test Match against Australia? If I had thought about it rationally then I would have realised that Trevor LAKE – not Laker – was, like me, aged five when big Jim routed the Aussies.

These were my earliest recollections of the game of cricket, and it shows how the game was gradually getting into my psyche. I could not quite recall Laker's memorable achievement in 1956, but I knew of it. I became aware that in 1957 the West Indians had toured England and they had a demon fast bowler named Roy Gilchrist who was a nutter on the field, not averse to bowling the odd beamer at unsuspecting, un-helmetted batsmen. But in 1958 I saw Test cricket live on the telly for the first time, when New Zealand were the visitors to these shores. England annihilated them because NZ were so weak.

England seemed to have no trouble bowling this hapless lot out twice in any match. I remember two guys who played for New Zealand, one being their captain John Reid, built like a blacksmith, with jet black hair, and huge white teeth that he bared as he struck the ball with immense power. Strong as an ox, he seemed to be carrying the fight to England on his own in the Test Match arena – and failing gallantly.

The other guy was an opening batsman named Laurie Miller, who was very tall, left-handed, bald and basically seemed as though he couldn't score a run. Try as he might he could never hack it in the five Tests and he wouldn't have got into any county sides in this country. I noticed his lack of ability and I was seven! This is probably a harsh assessment of Mr Miller as he was neither the first, nor the last overseas player to struggle in the alien conditions of England.

The following season saw India touring England, and they were sent packing as comprehensively as New Zealand the previous year after losing 5-nil in the five match Test series. I watched enthralled on the TV, as England racked up hundreds of runs and generally blew the Indian batsman away with our hostile pace bowling, led by the rampaging, ferocious 'Fiery' Fred Trueman. He used to rhythmically sprint to the crease, with his coal black hair (as befitted a former miner) bouncing as he ran, and his right sleeve rolled up but starting to flap loose with every delivery.

Then he unleashed quick bowling of murderous intensity on these Indian players, who were clearly ill-equipped to deal with such onslaughts. I remember India were so desperate that they called up an undergraduate named Abbas Ali Baig from an Oxford College to play in the Fourth Test at Old Trafford. I didn't know what an Oxford College was so I thought Baig was a schoolboy like me. Anyway, he scored 112 against England in that match and at least India avoided total humiliation as he led a failed, albeit brave rearguard action.

I was at Bearwood Road Junior School and my first summer in the Juniors was 1959, which was the warmest and driest summer in England in living memory at that time.

I was unbelievably picked to play for the school cricket team during my first year. An Under-8 playing under-11 cricket. I can't recall any of the games. I think I was probably too nervous to remember anything at all, but I must have performed satisfactorily, because I was never dropped from the team.

1960 saw me in the second year, and again in the team. I don't know whether I was picked as a batsman or a bowler but I do recall my brother, who was a wicketkeeper who could bat; well, he could play the forward defensive shot immaculately even if he had no other shots in his armoury, taught me that same shot in our back garden. Therefore I could defend as stoically as my brother. My Dad didn't play cricket, I think, probably because the game didn't give him any scope to get up to any of the dark arts with a safety pin!

Same again in 1961, the third year, although now I remember one game where I went into bat one sunny evening for the school at West Smethwick Park, and suddenly I was spanking the ball to all parts on the leg side. I scored 28 not out in double quick time and would have been accorded the Man of the Match award had it existed then. I can only remember I was exhausted from all that frantic running up and down the wicket as my score rapidly racked up. I was now learning how to make my mark in the game. And this was where Lightwoods Park played a massive part in my development as every waking moment saw me honing my newly found cricketing skills.

I remember with some amusement and no little pride one school PE lesson at Bearwood Road in the summer saw us playing cricket on our playground; and whilst I was batting I exhausted the teacher's supply of tennis balls, by spanking them all into the nearby gardens, which actually belonged to the row of shops backing on to our school in Three Shires Oak Road.

Those balls were irretrievable amongst the shop junk in those gardens. In order to keep the game flowing (or possibly because he was enjoying the display of batsmanship I was putting on), our teacher Mr Harris (yet another Welshman!) then produced a golf ball from his trouser pocket and had the bright idea of asking the bowler to continue the game with it. He tossed the golf ball to the poor bowler who duly delivered it to me whereupon I straight drove it back over his head onto the roof of the Infant School, cracking and bringing down several tiles, which resulted in an immediate abandonment of the game by the highly embarrassed son of the Principality!

The first cricket bat I ever owned was a Woolworth's Special. My brother expertly linseed oiled it for me before he would let me use it in anger. I promptly used the pristine blade to knock the cricket stumps into the ground resulting in deep dents appearing on the aforementioned virgin willow. He went crackers at me and rightly so. I learned a good sporting lesson that day on how to look after one's cricket gear.

Me and my mates used to play football in the park during every single opportunity we had. But in those impressionable days, once the Cup Final had taken place on the first Saturday in May, we used to play cricket; even though the cricket season used to start at school as soon as we returned for the Summer term after the Easter break, which could have been a few weeks before the Cup Final was to take place. And we, or rather I, quickly got ourselves organised.

We, of course, needed equipment to play cricket, and in those days Woolworths Department store, of which there was a branch about five minutes' walk from the park on the Bearwood Road, sold bats and crucially, cricket balls. These balls weren't real leather cricket balls, but were made of a hard rubber compound called Sorbo, and they even had a raised seam like a real ball. These Sorbo balls were the correct size and weight as real cricket balls, and didn't burst like plastic footballs disappointingly did.

I believe the twelve-year Statute of Limitations applies, and anyway Woollies has long since gone out of business, because we were not averse to shoplifting these balls, to ensure that we were able to take the new ball at the appropriate time! No wonder Woollies went bust.

My Dad made me a set of wickets out of some broom staves and he chiselled the appropriate grooves in the tops of them for the bails to rest in.

We didn't play with pads or gloves either, because no-one had any, so blows on the hands or more pertinently, on the legs were frequent and painful. There would have been many an entry in the scorebook 'Retired – In Tears' as a direct result of ball on leg.

My increasing obsession with the game manifested itself in my organisation of these ad hoc games. We would bat in a certain order, bowl in a certain order and everyone had to do their fielding duties. The pitch itself was our little miracle. We used the cricket ground-sized greenery which was coincidentally the area where we played our football. This field had the Adkins Lane side as one boundary (Adkins Lane Side); the bowling green hedge as the bottom boundary (Bowling Green End); on the off-side the two main fields were separated by a tarmacked path which served as that boundary (Hagley Road Side), and behind us the field sloped gently uphill and tapered to a point as it approached the Extension (Extension End).

We usually only batted facing the Bowling Green End, because to face the other way meant that the bowlers built up too big a head of steam on their downhill run-ups, and the batters were in danger of having their heads taken off by bowlers who had no control of where the ball was going to land, if indeed it landed at all.

Birmingham Parks Department used to do us proud. They would cut the grass on our outfield with the gang mower on a regular basi,s but would also turn up with the hand mower and cut the track we were using to make it look like a real cricket pitch, and also to give us a more realistic surface to play on.

My monopoly of organising these games of cricket now moved into the administrative class, as I organised one-on-one Test Matches, where, for example, I would play a full length two-innings match against another mate, where if one was bowling one would have to take all ten wickets before it was your turn to bat.

The games were therefore as realistic and competitive as possible, and very often would last three, four or even the full five days of a proper Test match. As I had been playing competitive cricket since I was eight years old, I was (naturally) the player to beat and I would use all my rapidly improving skills to ensure I was the best player on show! I had this vision of Birmingham Parks Department building four towering grandstands to make our cricket ground as fine as any arena in the cricketing world.

BBC TV were now feeding us a diet of ball-by-ball test cricket live on the box, so that we saw all the world's best players as their countries, from all points of the globe came to match their skills against England. These countries – Australia, South Africa, West Indies, New Zealand, India and Pakistan would tour England on a rota basis which centred around Australia competing against England for the Ashes once every four years on English soil. So we not only saw the world's greatest players in live action in our own homes on the box, but we would try and impersonate their bowling actions as we toiled manfully in our own Test matches in the Lightwoods Park 'stadium' we had created.

Players like Hugh 'Toey' Tayfield, the South African off spinner, would have his habitual toe-tap at the start of his run-up faithfully recreated by whoever was playing under the South African banner. The West Indian team was moving into an era of greatness and dominance, and I would replicate the arm-whirling drama of the quickest bowler in the world, Wesley Hall's run-up, whilst trying to knock my opponent's head off once I had let go of the ball. After I had bowled a spell of Wes's hurricane deliveries, I would recover my breath by impersonating the off-spin bowling of Lance Gibbs, with his characteristic quick-footed leap and skip at the point of delivery.

The leg spin of Richie Benaud, the Australian skipper, would receive similar treatment, with his combination of stiff-limbed fluency as he bowled leg breaks, that most difficult of bowling skills. But we could deliver all the different styles of bowling because we were so flexible, as rubber-limbed kids of that age seem to be.

During our winter, or the Southern hemisphere summer, we would fuel our desire for up-to-the-minute cricket news by avidly digesting all the scores in our newspapers, or listening to live radio commentary of England's Tests overseas if the matches were taking place during our waking hours. Reception from Australia seemed to go in and out with the waves of the sea, as we imagined a great long cable stretching on the seabed from Sydney to London. A player who emerged into the limelight in his home country would be eagerly awaited for our first glimpse of him, when his country next toured England.

One of my favourite players was Geoff Pullar, England's left-handed opening batsman who played for Lancashire. I followed Lancashire avidly because twice a year the three-day Roses matches against Yorkshire would be shown live on the telly. These Wars of the Roses encounters meant that I always supported the Red Rose as they tried to down the strong White Rose lot, and I used to will Pullar to succeed against Yorkshire as well as when he played for England, alongside what seemed to be most of the Yorkshire outfit who made up the rest of the England team. "A strong Yorkshire team means a strong England team" was the proud boast from these inhabitants of God's own county.

So much so, that I played a Test Match against my mate Rod Lucas under the England banner, and Rod's over-reliance on spin bowling meant that I tortured him over what seemed like several days and racked up 597 for 4, with my man Pullar remaining unbeaten on 291 not out. In reality there were only the two of us playing so, with no fielders to help him, and even allowing for our golden rule of no runs counting behind square of the wicket, his slow bowling meant that I repeatedly stood there and just spanked it to the boundary time after time. And to think he remained my loyal and faithful friend.

My penchant for statistics and records meant that these two prodigious feats of 597 and 291 were touted as world records by me on a tediously arrogant and repeated basis to the rest of my mates who, to misquote Rhett Butler in 'Gone with the Wind', couldn't give a damn!

At this point I really need to set the scene properly for these Test Matches. Let us take the aforementioned Test Match between Rod and me. For this match I had chosen England and Rod had chosen South Africa. If there were only the two of us around then there would no fielders, which meant that if the ball passed the bat then the batsman would have to fetch the ball and return it to the bowler. This didn't do an awful lot for the over rate.

If there was a third mate around, and he wasn't involved in another Test Match which could have been taking place simultaneously, then he would act as wicketkeeper. Any other of the lads who showed up would field for the protagonists. As there were no fielders generally in our games, then runs would have to be as true to the real game as possible. By that I mean that in a proper Test Match a single run would be taken only when the ball went some thirty yards or so off the bat when it found a gap in the ring of imaginary fielders.

Boundaries would be struck to the four sides as with the real game (except behind the wicket on both sides so it was to three sides of the ground in reality). Nearly all the dismissals of the batsmen would be bowled or caught and bowled. Obvious really when the only fielder was the bowler.

Leg before wicket didn't enter into it much, as there were no umpires, and if the batsman was struck on the leg it many times resulted in a lengthy injury break. When a batsman was out then he would take the 'realistic' walk back to the imaginary pavilion at square leg on the Adkins Lane side of the ground; and if the batman had made a sizeable score then he would receive his deserved round of applause from any of us in attendance.

Many was the time passing spectators, or even picnickers on a sunny day, who sat on our outfield watching our games, would take part in the realism of the situation by joining in the applause. Once the batsman had left the arena, he would dodge behind the hedge at the Adkins Lane gate and then re-emerge a couple of seconds later as the new batsman to take his place at the wicket. Exciting times.

During the summer school holidays we would have a departure from the norm by the visit of Bob Wilson's Funfair, who would take over nearly the whole of the grassed areas of Lightwoods Park during a period of about a fortnight, leaving us with a very small area in which to play cricket. Therefore our Test Matches would be suspended for the duration, as the Extension was also not available due its use as a funfair overspill car park.

This didn't stop us from practising the game, and I continued my reign as a 'flat track bully' by putting a couple of my mates to the sword in a very restricted area of short funfair-dictated boundaries with a golden hour in which I amassed 307 not out. The first and only time I scored a triple century, even if the circumstances rendered the achievement ridiculously and trivially unimportant.

I would print facsimiles of professional scorecards covering our own games which I produced on the beautiful old typewriter my brother had obtained from our vicar, Basil Westcott. As with the football, we would summarise the morning's play as we trudged home for our lunches in a parody of the way that Test matches were summarised on the radio. We, or more especially me and my AP Reuter-bound mate Rob Millward, became quite adept at this and we would then presage the afternoon's play with another erudite discussion as we retraced our steps to the park for the resumption of play for the afternoon in a style that today's pundits obviously copied from us!

If rain prevented us from playing then we would run through the latest episodes of programmes like 'The Navy Lark', 'Hancock's Half-Hour' or 'Round the Horne' mimicking all the parts and the dialogues as accurately as we could manage. We were, quite marvellously, locked away in our own world and anybody outside that small circle probably thought that we were all quite barmy! As I look back, I feel that as a young boy these activities at those times probably give me my most treasured and happiest memories. For Rob I feel certain that his career with Reuter's had its genesis in those fondly remembered days.

Rainy days, when we couldn't play outside, or late evenings when we were back at home, presented no barrier to my love of the game of cricket. I was one of many young boys who had a cricket game called 'How's That?' or an identical version called 'Owzthat?' The latter game was quite simply two metal, as opposed to the former game's plastic, hexagons which one would roll like a dice. (I have never used the correct singular of that cubic object which is a 'die'. It just seems like one of those anomalies of the English language which set one's teeth on edge! Proof-reader please take note!).

Owzthat could be played by two people, one who would bat, one who would bowl, or played on one's own, which naturally I preferred. The game was so realistic in a statistical sort of way because there was no physical activity involved other than to log the runs as they were churned out by the hexagon in a scorebook, or exercise book modified for cricketing purposes, as if one were watching a real match. I played this game at high speed, and it is entirely due to this game that I was able to develop a lightning speed at adding figures, and this mental arithmetic dexterity and agility stood me in good stead in later life when I worked in a bank.

Not content with simply playing 'Owzthat!' with no real purpose, I played a full County Championship programme between the seventeen first class counties (Durham were added in later years to make eighteen) and each county played every other county once, making a total of 136 four-innings matches.

I kept an up to date league table and, more to the point, up-to-date batting averages for every player in each team. This further sharpened my long division skills, as to produce the averages I did this all in my head, again at breakneck speed. I recall that Maurice Hill, who in reality was a journeyman pro in the Nottinghamshire County side of the early 60s was the best player in my Owzthat league, making the highest individual score (a double century, 217 as I recall) and scoring the most runs. If I had selected an England team from Owzthat then he would have been the first name on the team sheet.

That team could well have rivalled my England team of football playing marbles. Owzthat was mentioned on the radio during Test Match Special in December 2019 by the English commentators during the New Zealand v England Test Series, as they extolled the considerable virtues of the game and the intense enjoyment and excitement it generated. They said it was still available (I had my set sixty years ago!) and the New Zealand commentators had never even heard of it! What joys they had missed! Like Subbuteo for football, 'Owzthat!' is truly the prince of cricket games.

I did have another cricket game given to me by Santa Claus one festive period called 'Cricket at Lords' which wasn't a bad replica of the real game and was designed to be played on a tabletop. It comprised ten cardboard fielders who stood up on little wooden plinths. The ball was delivered by a wooden bowler, who delivered the small wooden ball at the little wooden bat with a catapult movement of his arm generated by a rubber band. This one held between the finger and thumb of one hand, and the batter played actual cricket shots at this ball. If you drove the ball against one of the fielders' plinths and he fell over, then you were out caught.

You could, of course be bowled by the catapulted delivery of the ball knocking the little wooden set of stumps over, and there was a little scoreboard with numbers which could be hung on its hooks. It was a fun game to play, but its only drawback was that if the catapult arm of the bowler was drawn too far back, then he propelled the ball either vertically into the ceiling or into some unsuspecting spectator's eye with the speed of a bullet. Protective goggles were not provided!

Our cricketing horizons were also developed in the Park by impromptu games organised by a guy named Don Badman, a name perilously close to that of Don Bradman, the legendary Australian who remains, statistically, the greatest cricketer who ever drew breath. Bradman was voted the greatest cricketer of the twentieth century by cricket lovers at the Millennium.

Don Badman would turn up unannounced in the park with a faded light green canvas bag full of cricket kit, and a game would emerge where lads of all ages would bat and bowl, and impressionable little Herberts like me would start to develop their burgeoning skills.

These days such an occurrence would probably have been stopped, and Don would have been suspected as a paedophile around whom young boys were not really safe; but I never saw or experienced evidence of this and my memories of these days remain joyfully unsullied. Sometimes political correctness does get in the way of the most innocent of activities, which is a crying shame. Nobody can take away the sheer innocence and joy of those days. Nobody.

When I was starting out as an eight-year-old in the Bearwood Road cricket team, my brother played for the Church team, Bearwood St Marys Cricket Club. They used to practice in Lightwoods Park Extension, where the young impressionable me would watch on eagerly, as the Verger's oldest son Ken Sandell, who played for Dudley in the Birmingham League, bowled at his teammates with express pace.

I remember in one practice session he hit a batter in the mouth (pre-helmet days) and caused a serious injury, removing as I recall, some teeth. My brother soon moved on to play for a serious club called Marlborough, who competed in the Parks league and were certainly not the equivalent of his Midvale United football side. Roger was a competent wicketkeeper who represented Smethwick at Under-15 level, as I had at football. He was a totally incompetent batsman (he would cheerfully own up to this fact) as he only had a forward defensive push, which he taught me, for which I am grateful, but with a bat in his hands couldn't hit the ball off the square, or in plain English, the skin off a rice pudding!

During the school summer holidays I would get myself down to the County Ground at Edgbaston as often as I could to watch Warwickshire play. This involved two bus journeys in each direction, and a rucksack full of lunch and then tea all lovingly prepared by Mom.

I would note every delivery from the day's play in my own scorebook, and would have enough money left over to buy a scorecard, which acted as an autograph book for the players, and sparked off another collecting hobby in addition to my collecting football programmes. The players were more accessible than the professional footballers, so it was easy to politely ask them to sign my scorecard.

In 1963 when Warwickshire were playing the West Indies touring team, the legendary Wesley Hall, now Sir Wesley asked me, while he was practising near the boundary fence before the game started, to fetch him a couple of icicles and gave me some money. I didn't have a clue what icicles were, but I didn't want to let down the world's greatest fast bowler; and somebody helped me out and saved the day by telling me that icicles were in fact the Caribbean word for ice lollies, so I was able to complete my famous errand.

When I was much older I opened the batting on the Edgbaston ground for the Midlands Club Cricket Conference Select XI against Warwickshire in a pre-season friendly; and made 10 in 45 minutes before tea, having cover driven both the England quick bowler David Brown and his colleague Steve Perryman to the boundary for two fours, both shots gloriously essayed through extra cover.

I could have kicked myself after being bowled by the last ball before tea delivered by the South African medium pacer Anton Ferreira, after I had easily negated the first five deliveries of his over. Tea was a miserable affair for me, as I had missed a golden opportunity to make a big score against a county team, after having a cup of tea and a biccie and twenty minutes' rest, before resuming on 10 not out.

I have already said that I was lucky enough to have parents who loved their family holidays, and the 1962 vacation was spent at delightful Bournemouth on the South Coast. Hampshire County Cricket Club played the majority of their home games at their Southampton headquarters, with occasional matches staged at out grounds such as May's Bounty, Basingstoke, the United Services Ground in Portsmouth, or Dean Court, the home of Bournemouth Cricket Club, when Bournemouth was still in Hampshire. The town is now mysteriously in Dorset after another of those nonsensical boundary rearrangements.

Our two-week visit to this delightful resort coincided with back-to-back three-day matches set at the Bournemouth venue against Pakistan and Gloucestershire. These started on the middle weekend Saturday of our holiday, with a rest day (to please my Mum) on the Sunday and then right through from Monday to Friday. Mom and Dad would drop the eleven-year-old me at the gates to Dean Court before the 11.30 a.m. start of play daily, and then collect me at the close of play at 6.30 p.m. while they had a lovely day sightseeing or sunbathing, or both.

As the players walked off at lunch or teatime, then young boys like me would surge on to the field of play to try and obtain autographs on the move from the reluctant, yet cooperative players. I particularly wanted the autograph of Derek Shackleton, Hampshire's legendary medium pace bowler, who was the meanest bowler around despite his veteran status. I rushed on to the pitch expectantly one lunchtime to block Shack's path to the pavilion and duly obtained his monicker.

Some fifty-five years later I put Shack's name into the You Tube search engine and to my utter amazement, found this actual incident of me approaching him in grainy black and white as someone had taken a cine film of it as it actually happened. It is to be found in a 53 second clip under the heading of 'Hampshire Cricket 1962 – Roy Marshall and Shackleton.' There I am, this khaki shorts-wearing eleven-year-old sporting genius, at 39 seconds on the clip standing next to another anonymous young boy, as Shack lopes purposefully in our general direction, motioning to an invisible man in the pavilion, in a vain attempt to sidestep this khaki-trousered human brick wall that stood between him and his lunchtime pint and sandwich. I am the one with dark hair, a dark top, and light shorts. Amazing!

This is one coincidence I still can't get over. It seems to be the type of event you will be able to recall with ease and relive when you have passed on and gone to heaven and are sat in God's auditorium.

I have this vision of Heaven being a giant You Tube facility where every event of your earthly life has been captured by the cameras, as it seems to be now in episodes of 'Silent Witness!'

I loved this brush with the professionals of the cricketing world as it seemed one could get even closer to them than you could footballers. I little realised that in the not too distant future I would be playing with and against some of these famous professionals as I moved somewhat effortlessly into the world of League cricket, with its grizzled old ex-pros and stars of the future.

And this idyllic summer holiday, my own personal 'Swallows and Amazons' summer was the time where I entered the Grammar School, not before I had captained the Bearwood Road school cricket team in my final (and fourth) year in the team. The games were not organised on a league basis, as were the football matches, so consequently were not as frequent as there was only one term in which to play them, unlike football which had the two winter terms. I have scant recollection of these games, but I was playing with and against players who would subsequently become team-mates in both cricket and football at school and club level.

Chapter Eleven – Cricket at the Grammar School

The upshot of all this was that my prowess as a cricketer was growing tangibly and I entered Holly Lodge Grammar School as a bit of a player, ready to show what I could do. In those days we all played football and cricket, as the chosen winter and summer sporting activities, and many of us footballers who were at the top of that particular game carried over that sporting prowess and were the best cricketers. School cricket was every bit as competitive as football, and the years at Grammar School held many an exciting duel as I continued to improve at the basic skills.

I played for the Junior School team in all four years at Bearwood Road, an achievement which I believe was unparalleled in the school's albeit unchronicled history. Which is another way of saying I think no-one else had done it, without anyone knowing whether they had or not. In the final year I was made captain of the team, which gave me the distinction of skippering both the footie and cricket teams. I don't know whether or not I was a gifted leader. I suspect not. But these honours were probably bestowed upon me because I probably knew more about the two games than my fellow man, or boy in these cases.

When in the last few weeks at Primary School my parents accompanied me to the Holly Lodge Open Evening and we were being shown the sports kit we would variously need for the winter and summer sports – football and cricket. Two V-necked football shirts, one with blue and gold quarters and the other white with a blue and gold striped neck. Two pairs of shorts, one pair navy blue and the other white and gold socks with black hoops on the tops, just like the Wolves.

But Mom was horrified when she found out that we would be playing cricket in white shirts, long white flannelled trousers and a woollen cream-coloured cricket sweater because she had to tell the disinterested teaching staff "Our Brian will never keep these clean. He can't possibly play cricket in white!" I don't think she ever quite got over the 'Midvale United Gaberdine Mac Incident'. The fact that her younger son, yours truly, actually had some talent at the game was completely irrelevant to her, God bless her.

I am not being unkind when I say that Mom had no sporting prowess whatsoever, her considerable skills lay in other directions. She couldn't ride a bike, swim or even drive a car. This led to some amusing incidents along the way.

When they were courting – now there is a word that isn't used much anymore - Dad tried to teach her to cycle and put her on a bike and she duly set off from Milcote Road. When she reached the top of Loxley Road at its T-junction with Wigorn Road, she promptly fell off, and leaving the bike where it lay, i.e. at the top of Loxley Road at its T-junction with Wigorn Road, stomped off towards home threatening never to climb onto a bike again, a promise she kept with ease.

I believe she said she could swim, although I never saw any evidence of this particular skill even on our multitude of visits to the seaside, in fact the deepest water I ever saw her in was in the washing-up bowl.

Driving a car, now see if you can spot a trend forming here with another mode of transport, the bicycle. When I was about seven or eight and we were holidaying in Weston-Super-Mare, Dad decided that the time had come to try and teach Mom to drive a car, as about twenty years had elapsed since she retired from cycling. So in our old Austin Seven, we found a quiet spot in the country lanes near to our resort, and Mom was nervously sat in the driver's seat receiving instructions from Dad. I was a helpless passenger in the back seat.

After much cajoling and gnashing of teeth (by Dad) Mom got the car moving forward at a speed that would have allowed a tortoise to cross the road safely and, lurching and sputtering, the car was hitting the heights of a speed of about ten miles per hour, when she suddenly opened the driver's door and managed to get out of the car, despite its onward trajectory and still being in gear.

Dad, not given to panic, panicked as he quickly had to get from the front passenger seat to behind the wheel and get the damn thing under control before the motor picked up speed and caused untold damage.

After bringing the car successfully to a halt, Dad was perfectly within his rights to enquire of Mom what the hell she thought she was playing at, so he did. He got the same reply as he did all those years ago when she said she was never going to get behind the wheel of a car again, another promise she kept with ease.

She never understood the importance of sport to me, and she was only trying to be helpful when I would walk miserably through the kitchen door out of the pouring rain to tell her that my cricket match that day had been cancelled, and she would say "Don't worry, I'll play with you". The sight of Mom coming in to bowl at me off her long run was something I could never quite envisage, as her soothing words had quite the opposite effect on me, and only rubbed salt into what was already an open wound.

Mom, although a gentle soul, was a woman of firm principles, and she and Dad only ever really had one row to my knowledge, but it rumbled on interminably and to my knowledge was never settled. You see, Dad only ever drank at weekends, because working in Coventry meant that his early starts and late finishes meant that he didn't have chance to go to the pub during the midweek. So he used to go to the Kings Head, on the Hagley Road, where Bearwood Road, Bearwood continued across the junction to Lordswood Road, Harborne traversing the major Hagley Road into the city centre of Birmingham. This was only a half-mile stroll from our house in Milcote Road.

Whatever time he had spent on Saturday mornings with his head buried under the bonnet of a neighbour's car, saving them a fortune in garage repair bills, he always emerged washed and smartly dressed for his Kings Head appearance. This usually involved him holding court, and entertaining all and sundry with his wonderful prowess as a raconteur. Saturday being football day, he would always be back home in time at 1.30 to eat one of Mom's lovely roast dinners, and get himself out in the afternoon to go and see a football match at either Molineux, Villa Park, St Andrews or The Hawthorns.

Not so on Sundays, and this is where the unresolved difference of opinion repeatedly reared its head. In those days, there was no Sunday football, unlike today where kick-off times and the days of the matches are at the whims of the fee-paying Television channels. Dad was not a churchgoer, but he always left the house late Sunday morning with the words "Just off to church, Marge" as if Mom didn't know where he was going and he was, in his own humorous way, referring to the Kings Head.

Mom would usually counter with her parting shot which was "Dinner on the table at 1.30, Fred". And true to her word, you could set your watch by her, Dad's and all our dinners were served and on the table at 1.30 to the nanosecond. We would eat ours voraciously, and Dad's plate of delicious grub would stay there on the table, cooling rapidly in his absence, because Dad insisted on coming home on a Sunday at 2 p.m. You would hear his steel toe capped shoes echoing up our covered entry, which was a sound-trap, and he would be whistling in time with his walking gait one of his favourite military marches by the American composer John Philip Sousa. You could reset your watch by his arrival.

The kitchen door would open, and he would be met by a stony-faced Mom, and off they would go. Dad pleading his case that he always wanted to come home from the Kings Head on a Sunday lunchtime at two o'clock, because this gave him a little bit of extra time with his mates before he started another long working week in far-off Coventry. Mom would hear none of this, and would state her case that dinner was served at 1.30 p.m. sharp. This argument used to be repeated week in, week out, ad infinitum, until one day I interjected and made the perfectly logical solution that dinner could be served at 2 p.m.; whereupon I was promptly told to mind my own business.

I think they were both frustrated lawyers, who liked the to and fro of the verbal battle that we used to watch on the telly in programmes like the American crime series Perry Mason.

As I said this disagreement was never resolved, despite my rather sensible suggestion, and I can still hear them to this day, neither one of them giving an inch. Apart from that silliness, Dad did his utmost to make sure Mom was happy and by and large I think he succeeded.

Back to the cricket. We were divided into four houses at Holly Lodge, and if one had a father, uncle or brother who had attended the school previously, then you were allocated to that same particular house. I was therefore allocated to Warwick House, following in the footsteps of my brother Roger. The other houses were Stratford, Kenilworth and Ludlow. Stratford were generally our main rivals on the sports field, with people like my big mate Trev Boyle striving manfully to produce victories for Kenilworth. And then there was Ludlow; well, dear old Ludlow always made up the numbers having been blessed with no-one who could kick a ball or hold a bat, but their house members could certainly navigate their way tactically around a chess board.

House matches were the first chance for me to show that I could play cricket, and because of the 'Test Matches' that I had organised in our park, I had long since mastered the art of batting for hours on end and delivering every type of bowling that a right-arm bowler could produce. This stood me in good stead as I started to make some runs in the house matches and take a few wickets with my bowling.

There was a beautiful cricket square at Holly Lodge which was situated between the two football pitches, and it was curated by full time ground staff. This was, up to now, the best cricket square that I had played on. The boundaries comprised the outer rings of the six-lane athletics track, which was creosoted onto the grass during the summer term circumventing the square. If you played for the school team the matches were played on the square, and it was something to which any young cricketer aspired to.

Being in the first year I was in the school Under-12 team and also made the Under-13 team. I can't remember whether or not I was captain of the Under-12s but I might have been.

We played matches against the other four secondary schools in Smethwick. The three Secondary Modern schools produced flimsy opposition, as cricket wasn't really their game; but the local Technical School, James Watt, this being the other school one could have attended having passed the Eleven Plus exam, had some decent cricketers. One of them was my nemesis Trevor Lake, (who I had once naively thought was Jim Laker). He might just as well have been, as I persistently found his bowling difficult to put away, as despite the fact that he had not grown very tall, he consistently bowled quickly and straight, and I began to fear his arrival on match days. I think he sensed it too, as he made it clear verbally that he thought I wasn't up to much.

I did have a good match for the Under-13s away against St Philips Grammar School one Saturday morning. After St Phil's had scored about 90 in their innings, we, or more especially me, my big mate Trev and the mighty Slinga, an under-12 who was to be one of the stars in the future of our Smethwick Schools Under-15 Cup run at football, knocked the runs off. I managed 46 not out, with a flurry of hard-hit boundaries for a nine-wicket victory. I was elated.

In the third year at Holly Lodge, or the Under-14s, I was promoted straight into the Under-15s, which was a very competitive year just as it was at football, being the age group at which football had become so momentous for me.

During our summer PE lessons, those of us who were in the school cricket teams practised, not in the school cricket nets, but on a makeshift track on the bottom football pitch, which because it had been trampled to oblivion during the muddy football season, meant that it was not safe for boys of our age to be playing cricket on. Because I was confident in my own ability, I decided to forsake batting and bowling practice during one session, choosing instead to keep wicket, and I let my ego take over.

My big mate Trev Boyle was bowling, and he was a left armer who could bowl with some skill and no little pace as an adjunct to his stylish and productive batting.

For me, showing anyone watching that I could actually keep wicket as well as being an all-rounder wasn't enough. So I stood up to the wicket as Trev wheeled away with his skilful bowling. Standing up to the wicket to quick bowlers is one of the most difficult skills possessed by seasoned wicketkeepers, let alone complete novices like me.

These days Under-15s are compelled to undertake this discipline only when wearing a protective helmet, in case a batsman gets a top edge and the ball flies back into the keeper's face. You guessed it. The batsman was defeated by Trev's pace and could only top edge the ball into my mouth, whereupon my bottom teeth, which miraculously remained unbroken, bit into my top lip and made an awful bloody mess of my lower face. I was a complete idiot and never repeated that particular piece of imprudence, not to say, stupidity.

Even though I was only a third year, or Under-14, I was promoted way beyond the Under-15 team, and was selected for a double-header one Saturday away against Kings Norton Grammar in Birmingham Under-14s in the morning, and the school 2nd XI in the afternoon, which would be my senior debut. It went rather well. I took eight wickets for 14 runs for the Under-14s, and then, waiting on the ground totally alone whilst I ate the sandwiches Mom had lovingly prepared for me awaiting the arrival of the afternoon's 2nd XI players, I followed that up with another six wickets for 11 runs in the afternoon.

If someone was watching me to see what I was made of, I had passed that particular test with flying colours. Fourteen wickets for 25 runs across the two games. I therefore bypassed the school 2nd XI, never playing at that level again and was selected for the first XI, effectively the Under-18 team, playing four years ahead of my time. There were boys in that team who were already playing League cricket, with and against professionals and even retired Test players, and I was pitched in with them.

One of my earliest 1st XI games was an away game against Joseph Leckie School from Walsall, and I was asked to field at cover.

The Leckie ground was blessed with a beautiful lush grass covering in the outfield, and I was mesmerised that as I repeatedly walked in with the bowler for each delivery, I was leaving footprints in the grass, just like they did on the telly. It taught me to always keep your appointed position and not to drift in the field.

Back at the Lodge I was now making my way in the First XI, and in one home match I was fielding at deep mid-wicket to our leg-spinner Pete Ashford, who was only a year older than me, as it appeared the school was building for the future. Whenever a leg-spinner bowls those tempting deliveries a batsman's eyes light up, particularly if he has no cricketing nous, as the batter sees it as a great opportunity to launch the leggie's deliveries into the stratosphere or certainly into the next parish for four or six runs.

One such brainless individual (bit harsh?) was taking strike against Pete who was newly introduced into the attack. His eyes, of course, accordingly lit up; and he smashed Pete delivery immediately in my direction, while I was minding my own business at deep mid-wicket, some forty yards from the bat, but with the ball doing about one hundred and fifty miles an hour as it sped towards me. As the ball started to lose height, I had two choices. The first was to burst into tears and call for my Mom, or the second was to dive and hold this thunderbolt inches off the turf and give Pete a great wicket. History records I chose the latter and suddenly I was engulfed by my jubilant team mates; and it was at that moment I arrived in the First team, and I never really looked back.

Chapter Twelve – Cricket Moving Through the Grades

Spooling back from my surprising, but welcome elevation to the School First XI when I was an Under-14, the cricket season for Under-15s arrived immediately after my almost unbelievable football season in which I rose through the ranks from not even being in the school football team in September, to signing for a Third Division Football league club, by the following May. Somehow, I managed to be ready to play cricket as well for the school, when we returned after the Easter holidays.

I was playing for the Under-15s in the midweeks and on Saturday mornings as well as keeping my place for a second season in the First XI. Our cricket master, Derek Morphy, or Mife as my Dad called him with more than a hint of Malapropism, came to the Under-15 XI with some exciting news. Spud (Spud Morphy? – well, we thought it worked), to give him his official school nickname, had entered four of us for the county Under-15 cricket trial match which was to take place at Rugeley Cricket Club. The county in question being Staffordshire, and we were to represent South Staffordshire in this match against our counterparts from the North of the county.

Besides myself there was my big mate Trev Boyle, who was a technically unhurried and cultured opening batsman; the mighty Paul Slingsby, Slinga, who was a year younger than us, an Under-14, but a powerhouse of a player, with his mighty hitting as a top order batsman, and a pace bowler who ran in and hit the deck; and another lad from my own Lower Five Shell form named Keith Johnson. He was a left arm spinner of some promise and a batsman who had one shot, the sweep, which he used to deploy whenever he had had enough of being at the crease, because he always got himself out whenever he played it.

Spud had booked us on the train at Smethwick Rolfe Street station on the morning of the match to board the Stafford express, where the four of us would be collected and put in a taxi or some school minibus to convey us to Rugeley Cricket Club. Three of us duly turned up at school on the appointed morning in the half term holiday with our cricket bags but there was no sign of Trev.

Time was pressing, and Spud began to get a little agitated and reasoned that I might know the best way to locate Trev and get him to the station as soon as possible as we were big mates. This was in the days before most of us even had land line phones at home, and a good thirty years before the mobile phone was invented so I suggested that we drove in Spud's car to Trev's house about two miles hence. Which we did, to be greeted by his lovely Mom, Doss, who told us Trev had spent the night out and she didn't know where he was. (We were fifteen years old. Judge for yourself!)

Spud was fast becoming beside himself with worry as he didn't know what to do, and was on the point of giving up on Trev and sending just the three of us to the station. I had a vague idea that Trev had been seeing a girl who lived in Bearwood and I thought I knew where her house was, so we duly pitched up at her address and found him, bleary eyed as usual as he had apparently forgotten about the trial match; or had at least lowered it in his priorities, pitched some way below his nocturnal activities. But Trev being Trev, he made it with his kit onto the train and the four of us duly arrived at Rugeley CC, ready to rock.

The South Staffs team we were playing for was run by an elderly teacher named John Bowdler, who hailed from Walsall and was obviously an ex-cricketer, presumably of some repute.

Not having a clue who we were or what our attributes were, Trev and I found ourselves opening the batting, with Slinga coming in at three or four. Keith was way down the order as expected. Trev hung around long enough to show that he was a nicely balanced and composed batter, but he departed. One or two more came and went, including Slinga, and I was still there at the other end, and racking up a few runs.

Before too long I reached fifty and had seen half of our team come and go. Suddenly I was there with our number eleven batsman, and I remember hitting a flurry of boundaries as I didn't know whether my partner was going to delay proceedings much longer by hanging around. He didn't, and I had carried my bat (batted through the complete innings) and made 87 not out, the highest score of my fledgling career. My timing in producing this innings was perfect as this was the county trial match, but even more so as quite extraordinarily nobody else on our team had scored more than two runs!

North Staffs subsequently batted and we returned to school to await the selectors' judgment. I suppose I would have had to have murdered the Chief Selector's wife not to be selected for the county squad after my score at the trial game, but thankfully Trev and Keith also made the squad as they had showcased enough of their skills to warrant selection.

Not so Slinga, who was left out, I can only think because he was an Under-14, even though he was a giant of a kid and, although he hadn't shown it at the trial match, he was more than good enough to represent the county a year ahead of his time. Sometimes selectors have to back their judgment if they are to be competent at their roles and recognise talent when it is there on a platter in front of their eyes. Youngsters like Slinga couldn't be on top of their game all the time.

Apart from the three of us, there were one or two more from the Wolverhampton area who made the squad, but the rest were from North Staffs, where there was a thriving League scene; and as the squad was being run by North Staffs coaches, there was more than a whiff of favouritism in the squad selection, especially as a couple of lads were drafted in from Boarding Schools outside the county but who qualified by residing within the county boundaries.

The first match was against Derbyshire on the County Ground at the Racecourse, Derby and this was the first time I had played in a professional cricket stadium.

My good form continued as I made 37, and Trev made a score so we were retained for the next match at home at Wolverhampton Cricket Club against Warwickshire. I scored about 12, and we were selected for the big away trip to Penrith in the Lake District where we played Cumberland. This was exciting as it involved a long trip almost into Scotland, and my Mom and Dad turned it into a little family holiday as they accompanied the team and I stayed with them after the game. The weather was typically dank in the Lake District, and the unattractive venue of Penrith Cricket Club coupled with a beating by the home county made the cricket forgettable.

All told we played seven matches for the county and gained valuable cricketing experience. I also received a salutary lesson, as despite my meteoric rise on both the cricket and football fields, I was still sinking fast in the classroom, principally due to a poor attitude and a certain wilfulness. 1966 was not only the year of England's World Cup victory but we were also at the height of the Mods and Rockers phenomenon amongst young people, and one nailed one's colours to a particular mast by the clothes one wore and the sporting of the appropriately fashionable hairstyle. I was a Mod, with a hairstyle which owed a fair bit to the Beatles and I managed to buy a few colourful clothes to further enhance my image.

The Staffordshire Under-15 cricket side had an away match against Shropshire at Whitchurch Cricket Club, and feeling complacent and not a little bullet-proof about my selection in the team, I turned up for this game wearing a bright red cardigan with black and white vertical stripes down one side of its front, completing my ensemble with purple and green checked hipster trousers.

It didn't matter that this outfit didn't match. I hadn't appreciated that I was supposed to be wearing school uniform, and the squad was assembled on the Whitchurch outfield pre-match for the mother and father of a bollocking which said that no-one would be allowed again to turn up for county matches wearing anything other than school uniform.

As we hadn't yet changed into our cricket kit, and I was sticking out like the Great Wall of China in a photo of the Earth from Outer Space, my public humiliation was deservedly complete. Or so I thought. I was allowed to take my usual place opening the batting only to be dismissed for a duck in the first over of the game to leave me the rest of the day to deal with my huge embarrassment and reflect on my complete stupidity. Big lesson learnt (one would have hoped).

The following cricket season 1967 collided massively with my O-Levels for which I had decided, at the eleventh hour, to work hard for in order to try and salvage something from the wreckage of my Grammar School career. Somehow I managed to fit in a full cricket season, my third in the school first XI. I now had my eyes set on playing Birmingham League cricket and my local club, Smethwick was the obvious place to go and forge my way in the game.

The Birmingham League was the first ever cricket league which meant that it was the oldest cricket league in the world, having been founded in 1888. Smethwick were founder members and had competed in the league in every season but had only won the League title once in its history, in 1951.

I was familiar with Smethwick's Broomfield ground, which was about a mile and a half from my home, and I had queued around its enclosed perimeter in order to pay to get in as a youngster on a number of occasions; and had been enthralled by the size of the paying crowd and the great moment of these League matches. I had also attended a half-term cricket coaching course at the ground when I was 14. Because it poured with rain every day, I never trod the hallowed turf but learnt enough indoors from the attending coaches to have my mates spellbound with my new cricketing knowledge when I returned to our home from home stamping ground in Lightwoods Park. (I digress here, but I have never understood why sports reporters always refer to a stamping ground when players return to a venue they used to play at. I don't recall them stamping on anything or anyone when they originally played there.)

I went nervously to early season net practice at the beginning of April at Smethwick's ground (I don't know how I managed to fit all this in, no wonder I placed my studies last in my priorities) and started to bat and bowl under the watchful eye of the senior players. They saw something in me, and when there wasn't a school match, over which the school had precedence, as with football, I duly appeared in Smethwick's third XI, the first two XIs playing official competitive matches in Birmingham Leagues One and Two. As the summer wore on it was, in line with my football, all coming together; and my football-daft schoolmates were enthralled as I recounted my cricketing achievements back at school on Monday as the only one of our year group to be actually playing club cricket.

Came the day when Holly Lodge First XI had its annual fixture at the school against Smethwick Third XI and of course, I had to play for the School. I was still only an Under-15 playing in an Under-18 team against an adult side, but I managed to score 56 for my school against my club.

This innings did not go unnoticed by the club and at the end of August I was selected to make my Birmingham League debut in Smethwick's 2nd XI away game at Moseley, one of the Birmingham League's powerhouse clubs. Curiously I was selected as a bowler, as I could bat and bowl with equal skill, but was down to bat at number eleven, despite my successes at the top of the order for school, county and club third XI. I can report that I bowled reasonably well without taking any wickets, and kept my place in the team the following week for the final League game of the season away from home against the newly-crowned champions of the Second Division, Walsall.

I was really worried about this as Walsall 2nd XI were probably, no definitely, the best cricket team I had ever faced up to that point. The morning of the match saw the game in some doubt as it had been a very wet week, and in those days games took place on uncovered pitches, which meant that batting was almost impossible against league bowlers of many years' experience who could make the ball talk on damp or downright wet surfaces like this.

Smethwick were put into bat by the champions, who seemed to have as much luck winning the toss as they did winning games, and we waited nervously as it felt like we were going to be thrown to the lions and thus, routinely annihilated. The crowd at Walsall were slightly more partisan than the crowd at Galatasaray FC in Istanbul and this august crew of elderly cricket watchers used to huddle together under the main stand, which spanned one side of the ground. This stand had a rusty corrugated iron roof and some years later I was to hit a six on to this roof and shower these miserable buggers with rust. Revenge is a dish that tastes sweet. LOL.

I don't think I batted at number eleven on this day, but I was in at about number nine, and I strode nervously out to face Gil Gregory, a middle-aged miserablist, with jowls like a bloodhound, who bowled at a brisk medium pace and made the ball perform unplayable tricks with the ball on wet pitches like this; and this one was treading water. Gregory hated a number of things – batsmen; young lads; and Mods.

I was, unfortunately, all three of these, and whenever I survived one of his depth-charges of a delivery he would stand facing me telling me in a Walsall accented Anglo-Saxon brogue what he thought of me, my ability and my hair. My barnet was sticking out from underneath my proudly-worn green Staffordshire Under-15 county cap, which incensed him even more as he was probably too old by about seven decades to qualify for the team (Ageist!!).

It would be in keeping for the self-confident youth that I had become to say that I met Gregory's venom with swift wit and repartee, but I was crapping myself and shaking like a leaf. Eventually, he put me out of my misery by bowling me a straight one, which I co-operatively walked past to be bowled and reminded by the bowler in which direction the pavilion was and by the way, did I realise I had scored a duck? Lovely bloke. Note to self at the time, don't put this berk on my Christmas card list.

We hadn't made many runs when we were all out, so had kept our part of the bargain in what was to be the champions final act of their title-winning season. Walsall started their innings setting off on what was to be the routine knocking off of our meagre and easily reachable score. Then our captain threw me the ball and asked me to bowl.

The pitch suited me perfectly and the sixteen-year-old me announced himself on the Birmingham League stage by routing the champions elect and taking six wickets for only 20 runs and sealing a memorable victory for Smethwick 2nd XI. I like to think that I gave Gil Gregory some of the verbal garbage he had given me, but if he looked in your direction you filled your pants, so I probably let him off!

In this month my school captain Kevin Jordan took me and another of my teammates, big Jim Edmonds, to Harborne Cricket Club. Although it was situated a couple of miles inside Birmingham, it was still within walking distance of home, the intention being to play Sunday cricket there.

Kevin, being a couple of years older than me, had been my captain at Bearwood Road School in both football and cricket, and was the school first XI cricket captain at Holly Lodge during this particular season. He was to become a rugby player and administrator in later life, but at school he also played in the school 1st XI football team at right back; and he took no prisoners in that position.

We never found out whether Kev was a good ballplayer or not, because the only thing he used to kick was the bloke he was marking, as he put his not inconsiderable weight into preventing the opposition from moving past him. In training you went beyond Kev with the full knowledge that you might have been about to lose the use of either or both of your legs, possibly permanently!

Big Jim was a left arm quick bowler who lived near me opposite Warley Woods, and although he had attended my two rival schools, Abbey Road Junior and James Watt Technical, we were nevertheless good mates.

He was 6 feet 4 inches tall and could bowl as quick as anyone. No less a luminary than Dennis Amiss, the England opening batsman and a man who once scored 262 not out against the great West Indies team in their own backyard as well as 203 against the Aussies in an Ashes test at the Oval, stated that big Jim was as quick as the county pros; which was a testimonial and a half.

Jim came to Holly Lodge for his Sixth Form studies before going on to University in Manchester to read Chemistry. From there he was on the books of Lancashire County Cricket Club and played as a professional in the Lancashire Leagues, earning a great reputation for his lightning quick, devastating bowling.

We both started on Sundays in Harborne's 2nd XI which consisted of me and Jim, and several Captain Mainwaring types who drove around in smart cars, some with cocktail cabinets behind the front seat! I was a runny nosed little working-class kid playing with these aristocrats and kings of industry, rendering me unfortunately out of my social class. Also, coming from the blood and guts of the Birmingham league I had a reputation as someone who would win at all costs. This was a totally unjustified and inaccurate observation, and to some of them I never shook off this label, despite playing at the club for the next forty-three years! I have a deep ingrained love for Harborne Cricket Club and one day perhaps I will put my memoirs of this wonderful club down on paper. Another time, moving on...

Both Kev and big Jim have sadly passed away. I was very close to big Jim, and he was universally liked and respected within the cricket world, and left an indelible reputation for us all to remember him by. Kevin always had time for a word with me and I was grateful for the support he gave me along the way.

1968 was a memorable year for a variety of reasons. Let's put a certain event of this year to bed right away. West Bromwich Albion won the FA Cup in May of that year. A lot of my mates who were West Brom supporters were elated. I am a Wolves supporter. I have acknowledged their achievement. This is my book. Topic closed!

I did take over the highly illegal school 'tote' in my final year at Holly Lodge, the rights of which I purchased from a classmate of ours called Roy 'Flogger' Laurence, who I suspect probably made millions as a salesman post-Lodge.

The tote involved taking sixpence (2.5p in modern money – in 1968 a not inconsiderable amount) off my schoolmates who would have the rights to a football team. If that team were the top scorers the following Saturday, then I would pat out a dividend after creaming off a decent profit for myself.

I ran a book on the Cup Final between West Bromwich Albion and Everton, asking people to choose the time of the winning goal, and I sold ninety tickets. The match was drawn at full time, with the winner arriving in extra time. As nobody had the winning ticket, then, rather dubiously, and to everyone's displeasure, nobody held the winning ticket; so I pocketed the lot! I know, I know, but I felt logic if not the law was on my side!

But 1968 also saw Smethwick Cricket Club win the Birmingham League for only the second time in their history, and the seventeen-year -old me had a part in it, albeit a small one. I should say that Smethwick's third title has still not come along, as at the end of the 2019 season.

I was now in my fourth year in the school first X,I and the most memorable event of this season was probably the funniest. At the end of term, the final cricket match of the first XI season was the School v Staff fixture, eagerly awaited by the school players as it was their big chance to catch the staff out of their comfort zone and stick it to them.

Kevin Jordan, who in a previous paragraph had taken me with him to play at Harborne Cricket Club, was looking forward to this encounter, as he had planned the scoring of a big hundred against the staff as his parting shot to the school in his final game as a Holly Lodge schoolboy. As captain he managed to win the toss and elected to bat, taking me in with him to open the batting.

Now some of the school masters could play cricket a little, and some of the other members of staff selected couldn't, so it was a motley collection of masters who took the field in front of the whole school watching and waiting for me and Kev to deliver the expected run feast.

One of the schoolmasters Brian Hadley ('Our Kid', as he was known due to his outrageous Black Country accent, although he could play cricket reasonably well) opened the bowling to me and in the first over. Mr Hadley was our Physics teacher, and we used to have a double Physics lesson on a Wednesday afternoon. Physics to me was marginally more difficult than learning Serbo-Croat, so I welcomed the classroom door opening and the arrival of PE Master Eric Quance with the words 'First XI' players please' as we had a full fixture list on Wednesdays.

This used to nark Brian Hadley no end and we would file out of double Physics with his exasperated words 'Yowm the bogs o'wind wot kick a bog o'wind' ringing in our highly-amused ears. A literal translation of that is of course "My dear boys, you are the bags of wind who kick a bag of wind" meaning 'Clear off you useless articles, how can football be more important than physics?" Answers please on the back of a £20 note!

On one memorable occasion Brian Hadley read out our Physics exam results and when he said "Robert Gilding twelve per cent" this was met by a hearty cheer from Rob. "It's nothing to be proud of, Gilding!" chastised Mr Hadley, "It is," responded Rob, "I've come ninth!" And he had! No wonder I wasn't the only one who failed every Physics exam paper slid in front of me.

I digress. Back to the School v Staff cricket match. Brian Hadley bowled the opening over, and I chopped one of his first deliveries quite firmly to the right of the gully fieldsman, and set off joyously for the opening run, calling Kev through. I looked on in horror as the gully fieldsman, our German master, Derek Backhouse, flung himself full length as the ball approached him at some pace.

Now Derek was a junior England Table Tennis international and had some great hand-eye coordination as befitted his sporting prowess. (His party piece was to play table tennis against any of us schoolboys using a frying pan!). Not only did he stop the ball but managed to sling the ball from his prone position to the wicketkeeper, who removed the bails before Kev could make his ground. In this his much-anticipated swansong I had run him out for nought without facing a ball. Kev stormed off towards the dressing room, pausing only to glare at me with a look which suggested I would be best advised to emigrate some time during the next five minutes.

The staff were jubilant, as one would expect, and their spirits were improved further when I managed to get myself out in the next ten minutes, so I began the long, slow walk to the dressing room where Kev was undoubtedly waiting to administer my deserved punishment in that special way only Kev could.

We had changed for this game in the Sixth form Common Room and Kev was standing there in his underpants having only had time to remove his batting pads and flannels. Upon seeing me he became incandescent with rage, whilst retaining the impish glint in his eye as he knew what was coming my way.

He grabbed me and sticking his hands under my cricket shirt, proceeded to give me a lengthy and excruciating nipple tweaking, which satisfied his sadistic humour and left me in a heap on the floor, with two nipples which felt as though they had been bathed in sulphuric acid. Well stuff you Kev, I mused quietly to myself, and thought that his revenge was a tad over the top; and removed from me any semblance of feeling sorry for running him out I might have had. What a git! I do look back over the safety net of fifty years and think how bloody funny the run out was, though!

At Smethwick I was playing in the 2nd XI when school allowed but meanwhile the club 1st XI had embarked on a remarkable run. 1968 was a damp summer, and the nature of the pitches meant that runs were hard to come by and team scores in the league matches were low.

Smethwick were led by a wily old pro called Jack Oldham (curiously, he hailed from Oldham!) who was a gritty, late order batsman and a swing bowler of great cunning. He was also a captain of bravado, not afraid to make telling and frequent bowling changes in a bid to bowl sides out before they passed Smethwick's meagre totals. It seemed every week that Smethwick only made 120 batting first, with a myriad of Oldham-inspired bowling changes leading to the opposition capitulating for 110 runs.

The local crowds were responding to Smethwick's unusual participation in the title race and games were well-attended. As well as the captain, the squad was built around two young and penetrative quick bowlers, Tim Hawkes and Paul Junkin, the latter being the older brother of my erstwhile strike partner Phil in the Bearwood Road footie team.

The vice-captain was a Welsh Hockey international named Gwyn Benson, an all-rounder capable of match-winning contributions; there was an agile wicketkeeper in Roy Walton, with his wicked sense of humour; a nuggety opening batsman in ex-Holly Lodge schoolboy Roy Freeman; a young Indian off spinner Ravi Senghera, who was destined to bowl his way into the Worcestershire County Championship squad before too long; and an old pro par excellence in the local legend Bernard Rowley, whose batting was always valuable, but who bowled leg-spinners of the most inviting trajectory only to see dozens of batsman succumb to his wiles.

The jewel in the crown of the batting order was the young Warwickshire pro Graham Warner, who was making his way with the county and was allocated to Smethwick for League matches. In August 1968 alone he scored over a thousand runs for club and county, but more of that anon. The first team picked itself if everyone was fit and available, and when there was a vacancy in the first team, I was called upon to step in, even though I was only seventeen. I can't remember the match, who it was against or where, but I was selected a second time a few weeks later as the season was nearing its climax.

It was a home game against Aston Unity, whose leading batter was Colin Price, a man who had made 85 in a Gillette Cup knockout game against the giants of Lancashire for Minor County Staffordshire a few days earlier. I wasn't called upon to bat or bowl in either of these games, but I was fielding at cover point when the formidable batter Price came to the wicket.

We needed to remove this guy to stand our best chance of winning yet another game, and before he had reached double figures he drove at a delivery outside his off stump, and the ball was scorching the grass as it screamed towards me. I got down and rolling over, came up with a tremendous catch off my bootlaces which was greeted with a huge roar by the home crowd, and I was soon swamped by gratefully ecstatic teammates. Colin Price looked at me disbelievingly as he began his lonely trudge back to the pavilion, but I had made a telling contribution towards Smethwick's title charge. Needless to say, Smethwick won that game.

The last game of the season arrived. Smethwick were away to local rivals Mitchells & Butlers at Portland Road, Edgbaston. If Smethwick could win this game they would be crowned champions of the Birmingham League for only the second time in its history; but first I had the 2nd XI game to play against the same club Mitchells & Butlers at home to deal with. In the 2nd XI fixture I was to be playing against the legendary, veteran England leg-spinner Eric Hollies, who was the man who bowled the immortal Donald Bradman second ball for a duck in his final Test innings at the Oval, when a score of 4 would have left him with a final career batting average in excess of 100. He finished due to Hollies' intervention with an average of 99.94.

In fairness, Hollies routed us, me included, for a low score. I went out to bat against him, and every time I played the ball straight to a fielder, he would move the field around a little and force me to hit the ball to where the fielders were now standing. Until the final ball of the over, when he threw one up in the air and said, "Hit that then!". I did, straight down the throat of the fielder he had positioned on a specific blade of grass seventy-five yards away for just such an occurrence.

Quiz question – what links Brian Jones and Sir Donald Bradman? Answer – both completely bamboozled by Eric Hollies. The upshot of the match, which Smethwick had lost by 5p.m., meant that we were all able to drive the two miles to Portland Road in time to see if Smethwick could achieve history.

M&B had posted about 230, which was a big score in this season of low scores. All Smethwick had to do was knock them off and they would be crowned Birmingham League champions. There was already a huge crowd in attendance at Portland Road as Smethwick set off after tea in their historic run chase.

It quickly became a case of whether or not Graham Warner could remain at the wicket long enough for Smethwick as wickets fell at regular intervals around him. But the score was mounting inexorably, and the Smethwick middle and lower order batters were digging in and supporting Warner. The crowd was growing all the time, and the tension in the air was palpable as Smethwick, or rather Warner, got closer to the required total.

Suddenly Graham crashed the ball away and pandemonium took over - Smethwick were champions!! Grown men cried openly as the club celebrated its finest moment. One guy, Des Green, a 2nd XI teammate of mine at Smethwick, said "This year I have seen West Brom win the Cup, my only child, my daughter Helen born; and now Smethwick have won the League. Nothing will ever top this year!"

I was still only seventeen, and had played in two games only, yet received an engraved, pewter tankard celebrating the club's Championship at our Celebration Dinner at the Blue Gates pub, Smethwick, and it is still a treasured memento. Seventeen, and I was already a tiny part of history.

The 1969 cricket season saw my final year at Holly Lodge, my fifth year in the school First XI; and I was now captain, giving me an unusual double of being school captain in both sports at both of my schools, Bearwood Road and Holly Lodge.

Was I a noticeably good leader of men (boys)? I doubt it. I still suspect I was given these accolades due to my keenness and knowledge of both sports.

I went on to play cricket in the leagues until 2010, providing me with a cricket career which had started way back in 1959, and I never missed a season. I achieved much in my cricket career and was recognised as one of the better players of my generation in the Midlands. As a footballer I continued to improve into my twenties before prioritising cricket and virtually retiring from the game at the age of about thirty.

Chapter Twelve and a Bit – My Youth Ends

My A level results proved Pop Haley correct in his summation of my ultimately abortive Sixth Form career. One success and three failures adjudicated by the Joint Matriculation Board represented a serious waste of two years academically. I had let Head Master Jim Thorp down one last time, and I suspect both were privately pleased to see me darken the doors of Holly Lodge Grammar School for the final time. I was not going to be a professional footballer, a professional cricketer, or even a trainee stockbroker. So, what was to become of me?

But first there was some serious celebrating to be done at the end of the A-Levels with my fellow students. As we were all eighteen years old and budding men of the world, we decided to pay a visit to the Dolls Club, on Deritend in the centre of Birmingham. This establishment was one of Brum's sleaziest establishments, and it provided a nightly assortment of striptease artists for the delectation (or something) of the local menfolk with whom we aligned ourselves one night. I don't think any of us had patronised a strip club before and I certainly hadn't the foggiest notion of what to expect.

They served alcohol of course, and after a few of these drinks we were as rowdy as the rest of them, and the rest of them included a bunch of sailors who were home on leave and spoiling, if not for a fight, then certainly some pee-taking at the expense of a gullible crowd of schoolboys like us.

The layout and décor of the Dolls Club was what would now be described in all the TV programmes whose subject is the buying and refurbishing of properties as 'minimalist'.

The rectangular auditorium, where all the action took place, had a bar at one end, dispensing beer as fast as the clientele could down it, and there was no seating, simply a few benches lodged against the walls, which were populated by the drunken sailors, standing on them and straining for a better view. What shall we do with them, eh?

There was no stage, only a waist-high partition separating the artistic dancers from their adoring public. Us lot, the youngest and greenest bunch in the audience that night for the entertainment, were of course, leaning against this partition, much to the amusement of those jolly Jack Tars on the benches. Sounds a bit like the House of Commons to some extent.

The house rule was 'Do Not Touch the Artistes'. Now, I am not a misogynist by any means, so please let me state pragmatically that the ages of the strippers ranged from about mid-twenties to, well, mid-forties? Me and my big mate Trev were leaning on the barrier, centre stage (!) and one of the strippers was standing in front of him, displaying her assets, shall we say.

As I leaned across for what might loosely be termed a better look, she put one of her feet on the barrier to give Trev, well to give him a more favoured vantage point. In bringing her leg up she kneed me full on in the face, knocking my glasses (for I was bespectacled that night) to the floor on her side of the barrier. Let us give her the benefit of the doubt and say it was an accident, although it was probably an oft-repeated tactic on her part to keep leering little Herberts like me under control on the barrier. I leaned over to try and retrieve my specs and realised that my nose, which had borne the full brunt of her manoeuvre, was now bleeding profusely.

This farcical scene had whipped up the beer-soaked sailors into a frenzy, and their comments on what was unfolding before them were full of ribaldry, and dare I say it, no lack of originality. My, my, what a wonderful crowd they must have been to have a night out on the town with.

So, as I was dripping with blood, we decided to call it a night and beat a hasty retreat out of the Dolls Club, consigning it to history. Somehow, the air tasted fresher outdoors again. Needless to say, I never dared venture into such an establishment again.

But my big mate Trev and I were not done, as we, along with a couple of our female colleagues from the Holly Lodge Sixth Form, had signed up for a six-week stint at Butlin's Holiday Camp, Minehead, Somerset as a holiday job to earn some much -needed shekels.

We travelled there in Trev's claret coloured Ford Anglia which my Dad had lovingly 'MOT'd' for him by liberal use of a roll of Sellotape! We got there and reported for duty in the staff reception office. When asked for my name I remember someone rather cleverly said, "But didn't you die yesterday?" as the Rolling Stones lead guitarist who I shared a name with had been found drowned on the bottom of his own swimming pool the day before.

Well, quite clearly, I was still breathing, so this rather futile attempt at black humour was ended when a female voice said, in a very familiar accent "Brian?" It was a girl from Bearwood, Irene, the daughter of one of my Mom's closest friends, whose family lived but six doors from the Walters family, of Dame Julie fame. Incidentally, I firmly believe to this day that Irene's Mom Ivy was the inspiration behind Julie Walters' much loved character, Boadicea Overall of Acorn Antiques, although I have still to obtain Julie's confirmation of this fact. So at least there was a welcoming voice there to begin what would rapidly become the most miserable six weeks I have ever had to endure.

Please do not be fooled into thinking that the BBC series 'Hi-de-Hi' was situation comedy. Oh no, it was a documentary, because after you had stripped away the comedy dialogue you were left with some dark story lines, all of which were based on true happenings. The four of us were deployed as bar and canteen staff, and I soon realised that there was some Black Market racketeering transpiring there. Maybe on a small scale, but who knew that? It was safer to try and comply with the orders given by these small-time hoodlums.

For example, I was working in the staff coffee bar, which had some advantages, in that there was a cigarette vending machine which would be in full use all night by the staff who were taking some well-earned rest and recreation after their horrendous work shifts. The staff would get Butlin's out of their system by drinking and smoking themselves into a stupor, and when chucking out time arrived, they would forget their fag packets, leaving them on the tables for me to clear up and pocket. Many was the time there would be up to nineteen smokes left in a packet so this became a little 'earner' for me.

One particular night I was working the doughnut machine which comprised a moving conveyor belt of cooking oil, and a contraption which every five seconds or so deposited a circle of dough onto the belt for onward transmission and frying. At the end of its journey someone would sprinkle it with sugar and the finished article would drop into a container for display and subsequent sale on the counter.

The people in charge of all these staff areas were ex-servicemen, who had been demobbed after doing their National Service and needed a job, so they washed up at Butlin's. The problem was that they thought the world owed them a living, and they collectively, to a man, had massive chips on their shoulders.

These were the boyos who were running these small money-making rackets. And one of these guys came in through the back door of the staff café one night, and sidled up to me on the doughnut machine. He informed me that every third doughnut ring dispensed by the gadget I should administer my elbow to it so that the ring hit the fat as a mis-shape. When these mis-shapes reached the end of the conveyor belt I was to perform a Quality Control task and reject them, placing such rejects into a plastic bucket, which when full would be collected periodically from the back door by my new friend.

I made some remark along the lines of "Are you serious?" when he got rather close to me, grabbing me by the lapels and saying into my face "Oh yes, very serious, sunshine. Now if you know what's good for you, you'll do this for me, or else".

Not wishing to find out what 'else' actually comprised I complied, and who knows how much money they made, probably in the town, from these misshapes. Utilising me obviously cut down on their production costs, and as I had no wish to be turned into misshapen doughnuts myself, I went along with it. I didn't have to nudge the gadget with my elbow as from then on I was shaking like a leaf anyway.

My other really nasty brush with these ex-service bullies came when I was made a waiter/porter at one of the holiday-makers breakfast canteens. These establishments used to serve up to two thousand happy campers who were breaking their fasts and one morning I had a double dose of the insanity that was going on which very nearly had me heading for home.

I was serving the fried breakfasts, which nowadays would be called a Full English Breakfast. These meals were not exactly lovingly prepared by the ogres masquerading as chefs in the kitchen, and I was called back to one table by a camper to whom I had just delivered her breakfast. She said "I am not eating this, look at the bacon, it is swimming in fat. Please bring me another." You will have to forgive me at this juncture and prepare yourself for what is by some distance the most unsavoury part of this book, but sometimes you have to tell it as it is.

Now because I was a good lad, I apologised to the holidaymaker profusely and went back to the kitchen and in a very nice manner, informed the chef that the lady on table whatever number wished to exchange her breakfast for one that was not quite so laden with liquid fat. "Oh, she does, does she?" he said sinisterly. "Watch this, matey." And he promptly urinated onto the plate, and then proceeded to blow his nose onto it. At this point I nearly vomited, but was quickly brought back to my senses when he ordered me to redeliver it to her at once, after he had helpfully stirred the contents of the plate around with a fork.

I was now too petrified to refuse and as I staggered back to her table, I was conscious that the chef and his mates were all peering through the windows of the kitchen door to watch the poor unwitting camper devour this concoction of filth. Which of course she did, and to my total horror, she even put her thumb up in my direction.

From that day to this I have never complained in a café or restaurant and never will. If there is something you don't like on the plate before you, don't eat it, leave it on the side of your plate and get the hell out of there as quickly as possible. Simply never, ever send anything back under any circumstances and ask for a replacement.

That morning went from bad to worse, or from the horrendous to the insufferable when I was asked by the chargehand, an ex-Sergeant Major, or so he said, to mop the floor. The vast canteen area was about as big as a football pitch and I had never used a mop and bucket in all of my tender eighteen years, so I set about my task.

When he came to examine how I was progressing he became apoplectic (and purple) with rage as he informed me that there was so much water on the floor that you could hold a "bloody swimming gala in it, sunshine!". He grabbed me by the lapels (a popular Butlin's move) and pushing me backwards slammed me against the wall and with an upward tug my feet were now off the ground. With his nose pressed against mine he gave me fifteen minutes to clean my mess up or else he would administer a sound beating to me, which I thought was a very generous offer. So, working at the speed of a Keystone Cops movie I somehow managed to learn how to use a mop and bucket, and avoided a thrashing, which of course I had fully deserved!

That was it for me, you could take Butlin's and shove it as far as I was concerned, and at last this six weeks of pure hell came to an end and the four of us headed home, each I think, mortified by what we had seen, heard and been involved in.

On the journey home I managed to drop a lighted cigarette down the inside of driver Trev's shirt from the seat behind him as we waited at a red traffic light in Bridgwater.

Naturally he reacted like a scalded cat, and the car shot forward as he lost control of the pedals, but he managed to save us from concertinaing into the car in front of us, with no little skill.

This was the second of such incidents, as he, when lying on the bunk above me in our concrete cell, (yes, it really was worse than being in prison), dropped his lit cigarette which went straight into my open mouth below him and lodged in my throat. With great difficulty I got the lighted fag out of my mouth before my insides went up in flames. No wonder I gave up smoking before I was much older.

Our return home from Butlitz (yes, it really felt like we were prisoners of war) now meant that I had to get a real job, and Mom was on the case. Unlike my three co-prisoners, sorry co-workers, I was the only one not off to Further Education, and that was of course my own fault due to my misspent youth. My chickens had finally come home to roost, and I was to pay the penalty of being left behind at the starting gate. I don't believe Mom or Dad ever realised the extent of my wasted opportunities that had left me in this mess, but in my absence at Stalag Minehead Mom, like the good mother she was, had been cutting job advertisements out of the Birmingham Evening Mail. She presented me with this pile of cuttings and asked me to make inroads into them.

The first three were adverts by Barclays Bank, Guardian Royal Exchange Assurance Company and another insurance company whose name escapes me. Now 1969 was a time of full employment for school leavers like me, and I obtained formal interviews with all three of these companies who were, I repeat, the first three adverts in Mom's pile of lovingly-preserved newsprint.

She also made sure that I attended these interviews properly attired. I think she took me to buy a suit, which was, of course, de rigueur in the world of finance. She even insisted that I had a tidy haircut so that I didn't look like I had crawled off the set of 'Hair' or 'Oh Calcutta!', to name but two of the controversial musicals bringing free love and nudity to the West End stage as the decadent sixties were moving into

181

the even more tasteless seventies. I am exaggerating a little, but you know where I am coming from.

How times have changed, because not through my attraction as a prospective employee, more a sign of the times, I received job offers almost immediately from all three companies. I was now in a position the kids of today can only dream of, and that was that I had to choose which job offer to accept.

Somehow, I liked the cut of Barclays Bank's jib, so I accepted their offer. On Monday, 15th September 1969 I walked into Barclays Bank, 313 High Street, West Bromwich, and so set the ball rolling on what turned out to be twenty-five years of boredom, little success, over promotion, disciplinary hearings, piles of paperwork and abject misery. But that is a story for another day. Suffice to say that Mom and Dad, and, I think, my brother, were extremely proud of me as my youth ended and I entered the adult world as a fully-fledged worker.

Conclusion – Misspent Youth?

Could I have channelled all of this energy, knowledge and achievement into an academic career leading me to a place at university, and a position in industry or academia, which would have seen me earn much more money than I did? I had a brain, and if I had channelled it in a positive way from the age of five I could, and should, have achieved far more than I did.

Yes, of course. It was a Misspent Youth, and while one side of me would not have swapped a single second of it, the other side of me would not have got involved with sport, but used my brain to, I don't know, change the world. When I see what some of my classmates achieved, then I think that could, no, should, have been me sharing that success.

This was my story. I hope there are lessons in there for anyone of similar talents to me. Set sensible goals, then go right ahead and achieve them. Between 1956 and 1962 I had few peers and then.... was it boredom that set in, after that repeated top year at Junior School? The years between 1962 and 1969 saw a rapid and dramatic fall-off in my academic achievement. Sport took over, and the sin of that was that I didn't fulfil my potential in either football or cricket. But once one is on that slippery slope, you need to retain enough active brain cells to recognise what is happening and arrest the slide.

In so many respects I was a lucky boy. I had loving parents and a sensible older brother who, although he tolerated my misdemeanours, never turned his back on me. I lost my Dad when I was but nineteen years old, and that certainly did not help me as I was trying to make my way in the world. My Mom I think would have walked over hot coals for me.

At football I was a part of our town's history. I signed for two Football League Third Division clubs and played on some professional football grounds. Cricket, likewise; as I played representative cricket and throughout my career again played on some of the best grounds in the country, as well as playing with and against some of the world's best players. Also, as in football, I was a part of cricketing history for my hometown club.

Therefore, in conclusion, if I could have my time all over again would I do things differently? Do you know, I think I would have done? Without a shadow of a doubt. I am constantly, even now, striving to improve myself, so yes, I think I would have done. Life has turned full circle for me, and for many years now, whenever I have attended courses or seminars to do with my work, then I have been the one who has digested every word and made copious notes, with not a trace of a facetious comment emanating from my controlled lips. I also find those who do chime in with Smart Alec rejoinders tedious in the extreme. Tout ça change!

To those I have offended along the way, I unreservedly apologise. I have admired the successes you have all achieved in your careers, despite having me as an obstacle during our formative years. To those who stuck with me as a mate, I thank you also unreservedly; and you will have your reward in a better place.

Thank you for your time in reading this book. Please do me a huge favour, and don't waste any of your own; life is too short and valuable. Otherwise you will have gleaned nothing from this book, and I want you to.